HOW MUCH ARE YOU
MAKING ON THE WAR, DADDY?

ALSO BY WILLIAM D. HARTUNG

And Weapons for All

WILLIAM D. HARTUNG

HOW MUCH ARE YOU MAKING ON THE WAR, DADDY?

A Quick and Dirty Guide to War Profiteering in the George W. Bush Administration

· Nation Books ·
New York

To my Dad
John Samuel Hartung
(1920–1989)

HOW MUCH ARE YOU MAKING ON THE WAR, DADDY?
A Quick and Dirty Guide To War Profiteering
in the George W. Bush Administration

Copyright © 2003 by William D. Hartung

Published by
Nation Books
An Imprint of Avalon Publishing Group
245 West 17th Street, 11th Floor
New York, NY 10011

Nation Books is a co-publishing venture of the Nation Institute
and Avalon Publishing Group Incorporated.

Library of Congress Cataloging-in-Publication Data is available.

ISBN 1-56025-561-7

9 8 7 6 5 4 3 2 1

Book design by Pauline Neuwirth, Neuwirth & Associates, Inc.

Printed in the United States of America
Distributed by Publishers Group West

— CONTENTS —

v

Contents

— PREFACE —

"This conjunction of an immense military establishment and a large arms industry is new in the American experience. The total influence—economic, political, even spiritual—is felt in every city, every State house, every office of the Federal government ...
In the councils of government, we must guard against the acquisition of unwarranted influence, whether sought or unsought, by the military-industrial complex. The potential for the disastrous rise of misplaced power exists and will persist.

We must never let the weight of this combination endanger our liberties or democratic processes. We should take nothing for granted. Only an alert and knowledgeable citizenry can compel the proper meshing of the huge industrial and military machinery of defense with our peaceful methods and goals, so that security and liberty may prosper together."

PRESIDENT DWIGHT D. EISENHOWER,
in a televised Farewell Address to the Nation,
January 17, 1961

"In this unfolding conundrum of life and history there is such a thing as being too late. . . . Over the bleached bones and jumbled residue of numerous civilizations are written the pathetic words: 'Too late.' There is an invisible book of life that faithfully records our vigilance or our neglect. . . . We still have a choice today; non-violent co-existence or violent co-annihilation."

DR. MARTIN LUTHER KING, JR.,
A Time to Break Silence
Address to Clergy and Laity Concerned, Riverside Church
New York, NY, April 4, 1967

THE CONVENTIONAL WISDOM at the June 2003 Paris Air Show

was that Donald Rumsfeld's temper tantrum was going to take all the fun out of the world's largest arms bazaar and weapons exposition, which is held every other year at Le Bourget Airport in Paris's gritty northern industrial suburbs. In a fit of pique at the French for their opposition to the Bush administration's march to war in Iraq, Rumsfeld refused to send U.S. combat aircraft to do flight demonstrations in Paris. And since sipping wine while watching the planes fly is considered one of the main pleasures of the show, most industry observers assumed that attendance would suffer as a result of Rumsfeld's decision. As *Aviation International News* put it, "U.S. Drizzles on Paris Salon's Sizzle."[1] My guess was that there would be plenty going on in Paris, with or without the inspiration provided by F-16s doing stunts over-head. So I headed over to Paris to check it out.

Aside from the deadly equipment on display—from precision-guided bombs and helicopter-mounted machine guns to top-of-the-line fighter planes bristling with missiles and bombs—the festivities at Le Bourget could just as easily have been a bed and bath show. There were plenty of free drinks and hors d'oeuvres, large stacks of glossy brochures at every turn, shopping bags with company logos on the side, and free giveaways ranging from coasters to lapel pins, all presented by well-dressed sales people eager to explain their company's wares.

Just as the Pentagon's prediction of a quick and easy victory in Iraq was wildly off the mark, the assumption that the Paris show would fall flat as a result of reduced U.S. involvement was greatly exaggerated. By the end of the eight-day show, over 300,000 visitors had come to Le Bourget, representing 168 countries, and reviewing displays put on by 1,856 exhibitors. Business was proceeding as usual, with or without a big U.S. contingent.

If the unofficial theme of the 1991 Paris Air Show was "how our weapons won the Gulf War," the theme in 2003 seemed to be "we can do business very nicely without America, thank you very much!" The largest deal announced at the show was a blockbuster deal by the national airline of the United Arab Emirates to purchase twenty-one masive, 550-seat Airbus 380A airliners. This was a huge setback for Boeing, which bagged an order of four planes from the UAE as a sort of consolation prize.

The Europeans were clearly enjoying Boeing's distress. The *Financial Times* of London sent a reporter to Chicago to interview Boeing CEO Phil Condit, who along with his fellow U.S. aerospace CEOs, had been encouraged by his biggest customer, the Pentagon, to skip the show. She filed a story headlined "Boeing to Stay in Commercial Aviation," as if the U.S. aerospace giant was so battered by the economic winds of change that it might actually consider pulling the plug on its lucrative airline business.[2] The article positively gloated about Airbus's newfound number-one status in the commercial airline market while highlighting Boeing's mounting troubles at home and abroad, from sagging orders from commercial airlines to accusations of fraud in its work for the Pentagon.

Preface

Phil Condit couldn't make it to Le Bourget, but I did. It was my first visit to the show since 1993, when President Clinton sent his secretary of commerce, the late Ron Brown, to help drum up business for U.S. aerospace firms by jawboning with the French, the Saudis, and the Malaysians. Perversely, both the administrations of George Herbert Walker Bush and Bill Clinton threw far more resources into helping U.S. companies market their equipment in Paris than the arms industry-friendly administration of George W. Bush was doing. In both 1991 and 1993, U.S. pilots who had flown combat missions in the Persian Gulf War were sent to the show at taxpayer expense, where they told their tales of U.S. military technology in action to rapt audiences of potential arms buyers. This year, America's arms industry would be represented by corporate VPs and mid-level Pentagon bureaucrats, a definite step down on the glamour scale from having Top Gun pilots as part of the marketing team. Joel Johnson, a VP for international issues at the nation's largest defense/aerospace trade group, the Aerospace Industries Association, complained bitterly about Rumsfeld's decision: "Is that the way to express your displeasure with the French—to turn the commercial field of battle over to them? . . . That's part of what's so hard to get across to our policy makers. It's not a French event. It's the world's largest networking opportunity of the global aerospace industry and its customers in 2003."[3]

Whether the French would "steal the show" in the absence of U.S. combat aircraft remained to be seen. As I set out to find the answer to that question and others, I was reminded that one significant difference between the Paris Air Show and a bed and bath show is its sheer size. The indoor exhibits are set up in a series of huge, airplane hangar-sized buildings. Walking through these cavernous buildings one is exposed to a virtual United Nations of world weaponry, with American, French, British, Italian, Russian, Israeli, Turkish, Czech and scores of other planes and missiles on display. Life-sized models of aircraft engines compete for attention with model combat aircraft mounted on giant stickpins. The Russian aircraft maker Sukhoi was running nonstop videotapes of its combat planes in action, backed up with a painfully bad rock and roll sound track. The European consortium, Airbus Industries, had a full model cabin from its latest airliner on display, and visitors were encouraged to grab a drink and sit back and relax in one of the seats. The Turkish Aerospace Industries (TAI) exhibit featured brochures and models of the U.S.-designed F-16s that the company produces at its assembly plant in Ankara, in partnership with Lockheed Martin. The Czech exhibit included nifty octagonal brochures with information on Czech history, culture, and economy, all designed to lure foreign investors to set up shop in partnership with Czech aerospace and defense firms.

Over at the U.S. pavilion, a very pleasant career Air Force gúy gave my colleague Michelle Ciarrocca and I a short tutorial on the capabilities and uses of the Joint Direct Attack Munition (JDAM) precision-guided bomb, which comes as a kit that can be attached to a 200, 500, or 1,000 pound "dumb" bomb to transform it into a precision guided munition. JDAMs have been used in such large numbers in recent years, both in Afghanistan and Iraq, that Boeing has had to run triple shifts at its main JDAM factory to keep up with the demand. There were stickers on the side of the model JDAM listing nine of the companies involved in producing it, starting with Boeing and working on down the list. I asked the Air Force public affairs representative if the bombs that are used in combat have the company stickers on them, and he said no, those would be painted in a neutral color with no markings on them. He expressed the hope that if the bombs got accurate enough, there might come a time when "we don't have to use 'em," presumably because no one would want to challenge U.S. interests in the face of such an awesome armory of precision destruction.

Fascinating as they were, the indoor displays were child's play compared to what went on outside. The runways of Le Bourget, an old commercial airport that was the site of Charles Lindbergh's landing on the first transatlantic flight, were crammed with aircraft, ranging from super-sized commercial airliners to heavily armed attack helicopters. Interspersed among the aircraft displays were vendors selling everything from an F-16 pencil sharpener to commemorative mugs and T-shirts. Beyond the "static displays," as the corrals of aircraft were called, were two long tiers of company-sponsored entertainment chalets, where the real business of Le Bourget is conducted. Each chalet consists of a dining room and bar, several meeting rooms where deals can be discussed, and a patio/porch area where visitors can hang out and watch the flight displays. The entertainment suites stretch so far out along the runway that many of the companies rent golf carts or minivans to ferry VIPs to and from their chalet.

After lunch, military men and women in the uniforms of their respective nations can be seen standing alongside arms industry executives out on the patios, drinks in hand, craning their necks to watch fighter pilots doing twists and turns, or commercial airliners lumbering up to flying altitude. On my first day at the show the flight demonstrations were led off by a new version of the French Rafale fighter plane. It may have been my imagination, but it seemed to me that the French pilot was being particularly aggressive, taking sharper turns and diving lower to the ground than I had seen anyone do in past years. People stopped in their tracks wherever they were to watch and wonder, either in awe, or perhaps in fear that the pilot had in fact pushed it too far, and might crash onto the runway below. It was as if he wanted to show the Americans that the French too, know how to play "Top Gun." The announcer literally swooned over his performance, asserting in the English version of his play-by-play that the pilot had "demonstrated the sound and fury of the Rafale." I muttered to no one in particular that the full citation is "sound and fury, signifying nothing." But by the shallow standards that govern at an event like this, I suppose one had to chalk one up for the French. They may not have fought in Gulf War II, but they clearly dominated the skies above Le Bourget.

While U.S. companies were cutting a slightly lower profile than usual, our allies in Israel had an "in your face" exhibit that was hard to ignore. From a mural depicting Israel's airport security systems to models of both U.S. and Russian combat aircraft that had been upgraded with Israeli electronics, the exhibit was one big, unapologetic celebration of Israeli military prowess.

The highlight of the Israeli exhibit was a video tribute to the fiftieth anniversary of Israeli Aircraft Industries. To see it, you had to walk up a ramp into a blue, circular, Buckminster Fuller–style structure. The room was dark, like a disco, and there was pulsating music accompanying an IMAX®-style movie touting the capabilities of Israeli weaponry. When I and my colleague Michelle Ciarrocca first walked in, there were pictures of women doing water ballet on the screens, followed by a quick cut to an Israeli missile blowing up a ship. Next came "the choreography of combat," with a bare-chested martial arts fighter in the desert, followed again by pictures of enemy hardware getting blown to smithereens.

While the film was flashing on the screens on the outer walls, the center of the room was dominated by a rotating object that looked like a mix between a vibrator and the cutting blades of a blender. It was neither—it was a scale model of "EROS," the acronym for Israel's earth reconnaissance orbiting satellite.

All these intimations of sex and death were making me dizzy, but thankfully there was a road map to the exhibit, in the form of the printed lyrics of the song that served as the sound track to the video. The mix of militarism, religion, and manifest destiny sounded like something straight out of

the playbook of the legions of the religious right in the
United States—maybe this is one of the reasons the
Christian fundamentalists in the United States have hit it
off so famously with their right-wing counterparts in Israel:

Our father in heaven
Give us the treasure
Power to rule the world with faith
To quest is to journey
We will do it together
And make the world a better place
Man controls air
Man controls space
Together, a crew, a dream comes true
We are the guardians of the sea
Believe in us and you will see
Peaceful silence, waves in motion
You can trust stirring ocean
We can touch the untouchable
We can see, yet invisible
Far or near
We see you right here
With a blink of an eye
We will be there
We would go to the edge of the world and further
Magic, grace, perfection
Power, pride, imagination
Creation
IAI

Although they chose not to do any big production numbers like their Israeli counterparts had done, the big U.S. aerospace concerns were far from silent in Paris. The Big Three U.S. defense/aerospace contractors—Boeing, Lockheed Martin, and Northrop Grumman—all staked out substantial tracts of real estate at the far end of the runway, not far from where the planes were taking off and landing for the flight displays. Lockheed Martin built two large buildings for the occasion, one for entertaining guests, and one air-conditioned, auditorium-style building for conducting press briefings. Northrop Grumman had a double-wide chalet, with weapons displays on one side and an auditorium on the other. The central display was a map of the world with pictures of various Northrop Grumman planes, ships, and missiles deployed on it. Visitors could manipulate a computer mouse and a touch pad to play "battle commander," flying aircraft toward their targets, maneuvering combat ships into position, and so forth. Hanging overhead like mobiles were models of various Northrop Grumman aircraft and missiles. And just outside on the tarmac were a number of actual systems on static display, including the spooky looking Global Hawk unmanned aerial vehicle (UAV), which has a closed cockpit that looks sort of like a bird's head to go with an impressive wingspan of 162 feet. If you asked nicely, the guys guarding the plane would give you your very own Global Hawk lapel pin and poster.

Although size certainly matters at venues like Le Bourget, what really made the American companies stand out was their slogans.

Boeing's slogan, "Forever New Frontiers," was the most

elaborate of the three. It sounded like a mix between a Bob Dylan song title and a motto from the Kennedy administration. And it came complete with a brochure that pictured a young African-American girl holding the globe in her hands. It opened up into a three–panel spread that alternated pictures of a rainbow coalition of smiling faces with airliners, attack helicopters, and fighter planes, all linked by the theme of "global partnership." The overall impression was of a sort of hip imperial power that it would be fun to be ruled by, at least compared with those heavy-handed Russians or those stick-up-the-ass Brits.

Given their marching orders to lay low, what exactly did the Big Three weapons makers hope to accomplish in Paris? Amazingly enough, they came bearing an olive branch. While it is all well and good for an ideologue like Donald Rumsfeld to insult France and Germany, referring to them as "Old Europe," that same arrogant approach just won't do for Boeing or Lockheed Martin, who want to sell airplanes to the French and Germans.

Even before the U.S. companies landed at Le Bourget, Rumsfeld's "ugly Americanism" had already taken a toll. Under pressure from the German parliament, the partner nations involved in building the first Europe-wide military transport plane, the A-400M, switched the engine contract for the plane from a Canadian subsidiary of the U.S. conglomerate United Technologies to an all-European consortium. Even absent Rumsfeld's rhetoric, there would have been domestic pressures to "buy European," but the defense secretary's fighting words made it that much easier to cut the Americans out of the deal. As for Rumsfeld's principal bête noire, France, the Aerospace Industries Association—the main trade group for U.S. defense/aerospace firms—made a point of noting in its newsletter that France was the biggest importer of American aerospace products in the world.

So, rather than pressing their European counterparts to be either "with us or against us," the American companies were more in tune with police-beating victim Rodney King's famous dictum, "Why can't we all just get along?" Lockheed Martin VP Bob Trice, a vigorous, bald gentleman whose head resembles a shining bullet, threw a dinner at the Ritz in which he spoke on the theme of "transatlantic partnership." The Aerospace Industries Association (AIA) organized a round table of defense and aerospace executives from the United States and Europe which allowed them to compare notes and plot a common strategy. "The central question we will address," said AIA chief operating officer John Douglass, "is what are the interests of the companies, quite apart from those of the countries themselves."[4] Beneath the surface, Bob Trice's call for partnership was just as self-serving as the Bush Administration's motives for going to war in Iraq. The main thing he wanted his brethren in the European arms industry to know was that he stood shoulder-to-shoulder with them in their efforts to get their governments to increase military spending, so that their armed forces would be worthy partners with the U.S. in future conflicts. Of course, bigger European defense budgets could also mean bigger markets for Lockheed Martin, which had bagged a $3.8 billion sale of F-16s to Poland just a few months prior to the show.

It ends up that the U.S. companies didn't need CEOs or combat pilots to fill their chalets and briefing rooms at Paris with reporters, potential buyers, and technology buffs. As the three biggest beneficiaries of the Bush administration's military buildup, they were in high demand simply because they have access to the largest—and fastest growing—military budget in the world. Reporters and potential subcontractors alike wanted to know how Boeing was proceeding with the Future Combat Systems (FCS) program, a forward-looking, networked approach to land warfare that will integrate robotics and state-of-the-art communications technologies. Likewise with Lockheed Martin's F-35 Joint Strike Fighter, the most ambitious multinational combat aircraft program ever undertaken, with eight countries buying into the program from the outset. The three main coalition partners in Gulf War II, Australia, the United States, and the United Kingdom, were all prime partners in the F-35 program, along with Italy, the Netherlands, Turkey, Canada, Denmark, and Norway. With eight additional countries already on record seeking to buy F-35s for their own forces, the program promises a long stream of profits for Lockheed Martin for decades to come.

Lockheed Martin's gain on the F-35 program may be U.S. workers' loss. The partnership arrangements involve permanently moving production for key components of the aircraft overseas. And once a country has mastered the production of a given F-35 component, they will be contracted to build that component for *all* future F-35s, not just the ones destined for their own armed forces. That means fewer jobs per Pentagon dollar spent at places like Lockheed Martin's Dallas–Fort Worth plant. Lockheed Martin executive Tom Burbage refused to rule out the possibility that final assembly of the aircraft could occur in parallel, overseas facilities, saying only that "Right now, there are no plans for multiple assembly lines. The option is there for the future." As industry analyst Richard Aboulafia put it in an interview with the *Dallas Morning News*, the workers at Forth Worth "should be worried, and so should management. . . It's a balancing act between market development and global and domestic economic interest."[5]

The question of whose interests are being served by the growing global reach of the transnational weapons industry is one that should concern not just workers in defense industries. Every American concerned about whether our national security interests are taking a back seat to the commercial interests of the big weapons-makers and their allies in the Pentagon, the White House, and on Capitol Hill needs to pay close attention to these companies and their governmental benefactors. The Paris Air Show is generally considered to be the world's biggest, glitziest arms bazaar, but that may be changing in an era when America's rapidly escalating military budget accounts for 40 percent or more of global military spending. The *real* arms bazaar is in George W. Bush's Washington, and it is open for business not for just a week or so every two years like the show at Le Bourget, but full time, day in and day out, fifty-two weeks of the year.

Preface

When President Eisenhower sounded his famous warning about the dangers posed to our democracy by the military-industrial complex, he couldn't have imagined the ruthless efficiency this political machinery would be put to in the era of Karl Rove, Donald Rumsfeld, and the Carlyle Group.

When Dr. Martin Luther King, Jr. gave his famous speech against the Vietnam War at Riverside Church on April 4, 1967—one year to the day before he was taken from us by an assassin's bullet—he referred to how the buildup for Vietnam left the anti-poverty program of the early 1960s "broken and eviscerated as if it were some idle plaything of a society gone mad on war."[6] The Bush administration's "war without end" budget poses a threat not only to the modest remnants of federal anti-poverty spending but to the federal, state, and local governments as we know them.

It is simply not possible to have a multi-billion-dollar, multi-year tax cut, a Pentagon budget that will top $500 billion by the end of this decade, a seemingly endless string of wars for "regime change" that are paid for through emergency appropriations over and above the Pentagon's massive annual spending, *plus* massive new expenditures for intelligence and homeland security, and still expect the government to meet its traditional responsibilities in the areas of education, income security, transportation, health care, housing, environmental protection, and energy development. This became painfully clear in September of 2003, when President Bush asked Congress for an additional $87 billion in emergency appropriations to pay for U.S. operations in Iraq and Afghanistan. The bill for the Bush administration's ill-conceived war in Iraq is now at over $150 billion and counting, a figure far in excess of what Paul Wolfowitz and his posse of cockeyed, neo-conservative optimists predicted in the run-up to the conflict.

When George W. Bush chose to use an aircraft carrier named after President Eisenhower as the backdrop to stage a "Top Gun" style landing in a combat aircraft before giving a nationally televised address announcing the end of major hostilities in the second Persian Gulf War, a Republican advertising expert gloated over what a great shot it would make in a reelection ad for Bush/Cheney 2004. Lest anyone doubt that this little stunt was a campaign photo op bought and paid for by U.S. taxpayers, the Associated Press reported that the carrier was repositioned so that the San Diego skyline would not appear in the television pictures, giving the impression that Bush was far out at sea, braving the elements alongside our fighting men and women. To add insult to injury, the carrier had to stay out an extra day to accommodate Bush's photo op, at a cost to taxpayers of a cool $3.3 million.

Is our democracy—the people, the press, the Congress—prepared to deal with the threat implied by this dangerous gathering of corporate, military, and governmental power in the same small circle of hands? That is the central question raised by this book. At a time when more than half of the American public thinks Saddam Hussein was behind the September 11 attacks, when 50 percent of Americans don't even bother to vote, when most Americans get their news from the "shouting heads" and slick sound bites they hear on

Preface

TV news, it's an open question whether the American public can rise to the occasion to restore and revive American democracy from the deep wounds suffered in November and December of 2000, wounds that have been made deeper and more serious by the policies of the Bush regime in Washington.[7]

Some of us were quicker than others to see that what the Bush administration was doing was different in kind from what has come before. Senator John McCain was probably the first major figure to notice the extremes to which the Bush administration was willing to go in using the military budget as a giant cash machine to reward its friends and punish its adversaries, when he described a $100 billion plus deal to lease Boeing 747s for use as refueling planes by the Air Force as "war profiteering." But McCain mostly criticized Bush's handpicked secretary of the Air Force, former Northrop Grumman executive James Roche, and the company that stood to gain from the deal, Boeing. He stopped short of placing blame on President Bush.

Paul Krugman of the *New York Times* was also on the case from the early days, but with a difference. He did not shy away from placing responsibility where it belonged—with the president and his key advisors. Early on in the administration, Krugman was describing Bush's approach to politics and economic policy as crony capitalism, American-style. As a trained economist, he was able to see from the outset that the Bush budget and tax plans were based on such bogus numbers that administration officials had to be lying, and had to *know* they were lying.

Krugman's biggest disappointment has been not with the neo-conservatives, who he describes as being like a "force of nature"—always there, always pushing the same reactionary agenda—but with his colleagues in the media "who should know better"—who should stop giving the Bush team the benefit of the doubt and realize that this group's overriding rationale is to expand and entrench its power and influence.

Currently, President George W. Bush—a self-described "compassionate conservative" who vowed to pursue a "humble" foreign policy—presides over a vastly expanded national security state that bares little resemblance to the government he took control of less than three years ago. The man who claimed he would modernize and transform the military while spending *less* than his rival Al Gore has initiated the largest military spending increase since the Reagan era. And lest you think that this change of plans was necessitated by the changed circumstances brought on by the September 11 terror attacks, please take note that only about 25 percent of the funds budgeted for the military since Bush took office have anything to do with fighting terrorism—three-quarters of the funds are allocated to carry out plans that were already on the books long before the Al Qaeda attacks. What the terror attacks did do was create a climate in Washington where no member of Congress dared question *any* defense appropriation of any kind. As Boeing vice president Harry Stonecipher put it in an interview with the *Wall Street Journal* in October 2001, "the purse is now open," and any member of Congress who argues that "we don't have the resources to defend America . . . won't be there after November of next year."[9]

Stonecipher's reference to a purse may have been too modest. Perhaps a bank vault would have been a better analogy. The military budget, which includes spending by the Department of Defense plus expenditures on nuclear weapons tucked away in the budget of the Department of Energy, now tops $400 billion, an increase of more than one-third since the Bush administration took office in January 2001. A new Department of Homeland Security has been created, and the budgets of *its* constituent agencies have more than doubled, from $18 billion in fiscal year 2001 to over $37 billion now. The United States has overthrown two governments in the past three years, at a cost to taxpayers of $170 billion and counting, *in addition to* the Pentagon's $400 billion annual budget.[10]

Since September 11, civil liberties have been put under unprecedented stress. We have witnessed immigrants and U.S. citizens being held incommunicado on unspecified charges, awaiting trial before secret tribunals. This has all been done in the name of fighting terrorism, allegedly to protect "the American way of life." This book is dedicated to the proposition that Americans will not let our democracy be hijacked.

It's time to take our country back. To do so, we need to avoid the mistakes that we all made—progressives, the press, and the public at large—last time around. Let's start by revisiting the scene of the crime—the 2000 elections.

Preface

— Preface Notes —

[1] "U.S. Drizzles on Paris Sizzle," *Aviation Internations News*, June 16, 2003.

[2] Caroline Daniel, "Boeing to Stay in Commercial Aviation," *Financial Times* (London), June 19, 2003.

[3] Paul Adams, "U.S. Aircraft Firms, Pentagon Are Cool to Paris Air Show; For Some, Losser Presence Is to Save Money, Or Is It Payback to France For War," *Baltimore Sun*, April 24, 2003.

[4] Anthony L. Velocci, Jr., "Showdown in Paris," *Aviation Week and Space Technology*, May 12, 2003, p. 23.

[5] Katie Fairbank, "Sharing Jobs on F-35 Jet; Lockheed May Allocate Work Among Foreign and Fort Worth Plants," *The Dallas Morning News*, June 19, 2003.

[6] Dr. Martin Luther King, Jr., "A Time to Break Silence" in James M. Washington, editor, *A Testament of Hope: The Essential Writings and Speeches of Dr. Martin Luther King, Jr.* (New York: Harper Collins, 1986), p. 232.

[7] "Delinking Sept. 11 and Iraq," *Milwaukee Journal Sentinel*, September 20, 2003, and Colbert I. King, "Baghdad, Birmingham, and True Believers," *Washington Post*, September 20, 2003.

[8] Steven Kosiak, "Funding for Defense, Homeland Security, and Combating Terrorism Since 9/11: Where Has All the Money Gone?," in Marcus Corbin, editor, *Security After 9/11: Strategy Choices and Budget Tradeoffs*, Washington, DC, Security Policy Working Group, January 2003, pp. 7–12.

[9] Anne Marie Squeo and Andy Pasztor, "Pentagon's Weapons Budget Becomes Bulletproof," *Wall Street Journal*, October 15, 2001.

[10] For up to date figures on Pentagon spending and related expenditures on military and security matters, consult the websites of the Center on Strategic and Budgetary Assessments (*www.csbaonline.org*) and the National Priorities Project (*www.nationalpriorities.org*).

The 2000 Presidential Elections— Returning to the Scene of the Crime

 **OH, HOW WE** laughed then! Those small gaffes in which Bush referred to Greeks as "Grecians," East Timorese as "East Timorians," Kosovars as "Kosovarians," and mistook Slovakia for Slovenia. And the coup de grace, that interview with Boston TV reporter Andy Hiller in the first week of November 1999, just two weeks before Bush was planning to roll out his first major foreign policy address. Hiller, a reporter known for his aggressive questioning style, decided to give candidate Bush a pop quiz on foreign policy by asking him if he knew the names of the leaders of four then current global hot spots.

The exchange is worth reprinting in its entirety, because it catches Bush in a true "deer in the headlights" moment, and demonstrates just how far he had to go from that day in November 1999 to his current position as commander-in-chief of the most powerful nation in the world:

> HILLER: "Can you name the president of Chechnya?"
>
> BUSH: "No, can you?"
>
> HILLER: "Can you name the president of Taiwan?"
>
> BUSH: "Yeah, Lee."
>
> HILLER: "Can you name the general who is in charge of Pakistan?"
>
> BUSH: "Wait, is this 50 questions?"
>
> HILLER: "No, it's four questions of four leaders in four hot spots."
>
> BUSH: "The new Pakistani general, he's just been elected—not elected, this guy took over office. It appears this guy is going to bring stability to the country and I think that's good news for the sub-continent."
>
> HILLER: "Can you name him?"
>
> BUSH: "General. I can't name the general. General."
>
> HILLER: "And the name of the prime minister of India?"
>
> BUSH: "The name of the new prime minister of India is [pause]. No. Can you name the foreign minister of Mexico?"
>
> HILLER: "No, sir, but I would say to that, I'm not running for president."
>
> BUSH: "But what I'm suggesting to you is, if you can't name the foreign minister of Mexico, therefore,

you know, you're not capable about what you do.
But the truth of the matter is, you are, whether
you can or not."[1]

Obviously Bush's mishandling of Hiller's questions wasn't fatal to his presidential ambitions, but at the time, it sparked outright ridicule, just at the time that his campaign was hoping to unveil the "new, improved" Bush, who had been training in a virtual foreign policy boot camp for the months prior to the "four questions" fiasco. And we laughed a lot.

But while we laughed and foreign policy pundits and the press "misunderestimated" Bush and his right-wing national security agenda, the arms industry did get it right from the outset. The arms makers put their money behind George W. Bush early and often, because they sensed that despite his talk of a humble foreign policy and his promise to spend less on the Pentagon than Al Gore, his national security platform promised a far richer harvest for them.

In my first public presentation in Washington after the selection of George W. Bush as president, I referred to an article that I had read about a son whose father had been president of certain country, and who had recently risen to the presidency of that same nation under suspicious circumstances. The punch line to my little joke was that the article was about the ascendance of Joseph Mobutu to the presidency of the Democratic Republic of the Congo, *not* the ascendance of George W. Bush to the presidency of the United States.

A few of the assembled members of the press corps

chuckled. A larger number clucked their tongues at the thought anyone would even *joke* at the idea that *our democratic system* could be compared to a Third World junta. But as time goes by and our liberties are further eroded by military decrees, anti-terror laws, and persistent bullying and browbeating by the likes of Donald Rumsfeld and John Ashcroft, I have to wonder if the day will come when such a comparison will no longer be a joke, but an uncomfortable metaphor for contemporary American political reality.

The 2000 elections mark an important moment in the transformation of America from a republic, in which the military and security forces are subordinated to civilian control, into a garrison state, in which the security of the state and the corporation take precedence over the rights of the individual.

Why didn't we see this coming? Why didn't we realize that George W. Bush was a radical, right-wing, neo-conservative "wolf" dressed up in compassionate conservative "sheep's" clothing? Was George W. Bush *that good* a communicator, or were we missing the forest for the trees? Did American voters get "rope-a-doped" by the Bush campaign? The answer lies in the discrepancies between Bush as candidate and as president on foreign policy, as revealed by his choice of campaign advisors, major speeches, and debate performances.

The same "compassionate conservative" dichotomy that exists in his domestic policy agenda also exists in his foreign policy pronouncements. In campaign mode, Bush preferred the iron fist to be hidden beneath a velvet glove, so as not to scare off the soccer moms and other swing voters he would need to build an electoral majority. He often papered over just how radical his foreign policy agenda was, to the point that even fairly sophisticated analysts were lulled into a false sense of security, assuming that he would be a slightly more conservative version of his father, perhaps with a stronger isolationist streak. Few expected Bush to go out into the world seeking monsters to slay, and trying to remake the map of the world by force.

The foreign policy tag line that most remember from Bush's campaign was that the United States should be a "humble nation," and avoid involvement in "aimless and endless deployments" or well-meaning but resource-draining nation building projects like the one the Clinton administration had undertaken in the Balkans.

The notion that Bush might steer clear of foreign affairs was reinforced by his first, tentative forays into the topic, which were so disastrous that they made him grist for humor columnists and late night comedians.

At the *Washington Post*, the editorial page was more forgiving with regard to Bush's lack of mastery of the names of foreign leaders, noting that "we don't think George W. Bush is going to lose many votes because he can't name the leader of Chechnya." The *Post* reiterated the point made by Bush spokesperson Karen Hughes, that "for the American people, the relevant question isn't how many names of foreign leaders a candidate knows, but whether he has a strategic vision for America's role in the world." But it was precisely here, on the question of America's role in relationship to other nations, that the *Post* editors took pause. Despite some uncertainty about *who* was running Pakistan, Bush managed to slip out of his deer-in-the-headlights posture long enough to endorse the notion that a general taking power there in a military coup would "bring stability to the country" and be "good news for the subcontinent." The *Post* begged to differ, noting that over time, democracies are far more conducive to stability than military-dominated regimes, and that promoting democracy and human rights should be at the center of the United States' strategic vision of its role in the world. Washington's newspaper of record ended by saying "We'd like to hear more from Mr. Bush—and this time it could be on a take home exam—about where democracy fits in his strategic vision of the world."[2]

The *Post* was right to highlight the question of where candidate Bush stood on issues of democracy and human rights. Three years and two regimes changes later, it's still not entirely clear where these critical issues fit into President George W. Bush's world view. The governments that his administration displaced in Afghanistan and Iraq were clearly tyrannies, but the regimes the United States has helped to install in their place are democracies in name only, lacking either the mechanisms for popular input and accountability or the institutional underpinnings essential to a genuine democratic state. And some of the president's closest allies in his self-declared "war on terrorism," from the Saudi monarchy to the Uzbek dictatorship to the military regime of General Musharraf in Pakistan ("the general" of Bush's answer back in November 1999), are among the most repressive rulers on the planet.

But how did Bush get from there to here? Who did he turn to for help with his "foreign policy attention deficit disorder"?

Enter the Vulcans

When then Texas Governor Ann Richards was warming up the Democratic faithful at the party's 1988 nominating convention, she attacked the Republican candidate, George Herbert Walker Bush, as a child of privilege who was "born on third base and thought he hit a triple."

Richards' rhetorical flourish applies even more persuasively to the son than to the father. When George W. Bush started out his campaign, he had far higher name recognition than any of his rivals, *in large part because most of the people polled thought he was his father*. It was not until well into his campaign for the presidency—and his fundraising effort—that pollsters found the appropriate techniques to inform the people being surveyed that they were asking about *another* George Bush.

Likewise, when it became clear that George W. Bush needed some serious schooling in foreign affairs, Dad was able to help out.

It all started in the summer of 1998 at the Bush family compound in Kennebunkport, Maine, when Bush the elder introduced Bush the younger to Condoleezza ("Condi") Rice, a specialist on the former Soviet Union who had served on the National Security Council under Brent Scowcroft in the Bush administration. According to an account by John Lancaster and Terry Neal for the *Washington Post,* Condi

Rice and George W. Bush had discussions over several days at the Kennebunkport compound, and they hit it off well enough that Rice agreed to head up a foreign policy advisory team for Bush.

The team that Rice assembled, with the help of Papa Bush, was a formidable one. It included Richard Armitage, a former assistant secretary of defense in the Reagan administration; Robert Blackwill, a national security council staffer in the Bush the elder administration; Stephen Hadley, a lawyer and an assistant secretary of defense in the Bush administration; Richard Perle, an assistant secretary of defense in the Reagan administration; Paul Wolfowitz, dean of the Johns Hopkins School of Advanced International Studies and an undersecretary of defense in the Bush administration; Dov Zakheim, a deputy undersecretary of defense in the Bush administration; and Robert Zoellick, deputy chief of staff in the Bush White House.

The group called itself "the Vulcans," after the Roman god of fire and metalworking. The name was chosen in honor of Rice's home town of Birmingham, Alabama, a steel town which has a prominent statue of the god Vulcan on display within its environs. Their job was to "forge" a coherent foreign policy for the George W. Bush administration in-the-making; the question would be in which sense of the term: forge, as in shape, in the metalworking sense; or forge, as in fabricate, distort, or lie, in the sense of a grand deception? And perhaps most importantly of all, how much of the final product would be George W. Bush, and how much would be the handiwork of his Republican handlers, however skilled and experienced a group they might be?

Superficially, the Vulcans appeared to be a balanced representation of the Republican party, not dissimilar from the kind of group Bush's father might have assembled. Rice was a protégé of Brent Scowcroft, a moderate internationalist who was intimately involved in negotiating arms reductions with Moscow and encouraging a peaceful dissolution of the Soviet empire. Rice's association with Scowcroft, and a brief earlier stint as an advisor to Gary Hart's ill-fated 1988 presidential campaign, marked her as moderate Republican, not an aggressive neo-conservative of the kind that has come to dominate policy-making in the George W. Bush administration.

The neo-conservative "camp" within the Vulcans was led by Paul Wolfowitz. He had helped to draft a unilateralist national security strategy at the Pentagon during Bush the elder's administration, only to have it watered down after complaints from moderates like Colin Powell, Scowcroft, and President Bush himself. Wolfowitz served as almost a de facto co-chair of the advisory group alongside Rice. The other main neo-conservative voice was Richard Perle's, the neo-con's neo-con, known as "the Prince of Darkness" during the Reagan administration for his gloom-and-doom views of Soviet capabilities and intentions.

While Wolfowitz and Perle represented strong neo-conservative voices, they were countered not only by Rice but by Dov Zakheim, a former Pentagon official who was less interested in ideology than he was in genuine defense reform. Zakheim was one of the people pushing Bush to consider a leaner, meaner military based on fewer big, cumbersome, costly weapons platforms. Robert Zoellick was another moderate on the Vulcan roster. A committed free trader, Zoellick had spent some of his time out of government at Fannie Mae, the federally-chartered home mortgage agency that is now under heavy fire from conservatives in Congress.

Rounding out George W. Bush's foreign policy advisory group were heavy hitters like George Shultz, who steered Ronald Reagan down the road of deep nuclear arms reductions as his secretary of state in the 1980s; and Colin Powell, who, although not formally a "Vulcan," helped Bush during his campaign and frequently appeared with him at campaign events.

Richard Armitage, a moderate who ended up as Colin Powell's deputy at the State Department after turning down the chance to be Donald Rumsfeld's second-in-charge at the Pentagon (allegedly, according to one insider, because he thinks Rumsfeld is "a prick"), also served as a Vulcan. Robert Blackwill, an academic and former Bush administration National Security Council aide, was also on the team, as was Stephen Hadley, a bright, mostly non-ideological conservative with radical ideas about how to revise U.S.-Russian nuclear relations.

While the moderates or "non-ideologues"—Condi Rice, Dick Armitage, Dov Zakheim, Bob Zoellick, George Schultz, and Colin Powell—appeared to outnumber the neo-conservative hawks like Paul Wolfowitz and Richard Perle on the Bush foreign policy advisory team, the predisposition of "Dubya" greatly affected how he interpreted and used the advice that he received.

When it comes to foreign policy, George W. Bush is clearly *not* his father's son. George Herbert Walker Bush came to the presidency with considerable foreign policy experience, having served as CIA director and ambassador to China and as vice president to Ronald Reagan, who was one of the most activist presidents on foreign policy in living memory. By contrast, George W. Bush had a reputation as a playboy, and had shown little interest in politics in general or foreign affairs in particular until late in life. Before running for Governor of Texas, his foreign experiences were limited to the occasional ceremonial trip on his father's behalf to Ghana, or China, while his father was ambassador there and where young Bush indicated that his main goal was to "meet babes." During the campaign, Bush and his advisors tried to make much of the fact that as governor of Texas he had developed a relationship with Mexican president Vicente Fox, in a sort of "Tex-Mex foreign policy."

So, for the most part, Bush the younger appeared to be a blank slate on foreign policy. Aside from a strong interest in missile defense, which he reiterated at every opportunity, there was no unifying theme to his foreign policy preferences, nor did he express any strong interest in international affairs. *Newsweek* columnist Jonathan Alter, who had the opportunity to meet George W. Bush during the 2000 campaign, described him as not so much unintelligent on foreign affairs as disinterested, leading Alter to refer to Bush as "incurious George."

Because of Bush's lack of experience, the question of who was advising him, and whether Bush was merely parroting lines fed to him by his advisors, became paramount. In a piece that ran in the *Washington Post* on November 19, 2000, the day that Bush gave his first major foreign policy address at the Ronald Reagan Library in Simi Valley, California, correspondents John Lancaster and Terry Neal raised this sensitive subject with a Bush advisor: "The Vulcans are understandably sensitive to suggestions that Bush is reading from a script. Asked to name a specific case in which Bush overruled his advisers, one of them said: 'You mean, does he have a brain?'"

As it turned out, the Vulcans were hard pressed to come up with an example in which Bush *had* overruled them. What they did come up with was revealing, however. As one adviser put it, Bush's style wasn't so much "rejecting the consensus of the group as it is pushing the group to be a little bolder."

On the relationship between missile defense and the Anti-Ballistic Missile treaty—which many international diplomats have seen as a cornerstone of the global nuclear arms control regime—one Vulcan told Lancaster and Neal that "All of us to a greater or lesser extent were uncomfortable with the treaty, but Bush said 'My concern isn't the treaty. My concern is [building a] missile defense, and I don't want anything to stand in the way of it.'"

Another "innovation" that his advisers attributed to Bush was the decision to call China a "strategic competitor" instead of a "strategic partner." This move threw U.S.-China relations into disarray in the early months of his administration during the mini-crisis over Beijing's downing of a U.S.

spy plane, and continues to cause confusion as to whether the Bush foreign policy team sees China primarily as a "market" or a "menace." Diplomats and military personnel with expertise in Asia have argued that describing China as the enemy of the future could become a self-fulfilling prophecy. The wiser course would be to manage the U.S.-China relationship—through trade, political and security exchanges—thus reducing the likelihood of a confrontational relationship ten or twenty years from now. The phrase "strategic competitor" may please "peace through strength" advocates like Frank Gaffney of the ultra-right Center for Security Policy, but it is not at all clear that it serves U.S. security interests in either the short- or longer-term.

Another instinct that Bush revealed in meetings with the Vulcans was expressed in his bold question: "Why do we need an Army?" On the one hand, this could show a reformist instinct. Given the immense superiority the U.S. armed forces have over most of the adversaries they have faced in the past decade—from Slobodan Milosevic's Serbian militias, to the Taliban, to Saddam Hussein's Republican Guard—it makes perfect sense to ask hard questions about how much heavy armor is needed to augment the U.S. military's obvious and growing air superiority. However, it seems more likely that the instinct that Bush revealed with this question was an anti-Army, pro-Air Force bias, a view shared by Donald Rumsfeld and Paul Wolfowitz. This profound lack of respect for the realities of ground combat has contributed to the disastrously bad planning that "Team Bush" engaged in prior to the occupation of Iraq.

The final example of Bush's foreign policy judgment that leaked out early in the campaign relates to his position on nuclear weapons testing. In what one of his advisors described as a fair and balanced compromise, the team took the advice of Stephen Hadley, a Vulcan who later worked for Condi Rice at the National Security Council after Bush was selected president. Hadley suggested that the Bush campaign should oppose the Comprehensive Test Ban, a treaty with massive international support that calls for an end to underground testing of nuclear bombs—above-ground tests are already banned under a treaty developed during the Kennedy administration—but that it should maintain the voluntary U.S. moratorium on nuclear testing that had been in place for some years. Looked at in hindsight, this compromise is vintage Bush: It gives the United States maximum freedom of action with the minimum level of accountability. It undermines a major international agreement that would have a binding impact on scores of nations while allowing the United States to posture as a "good guy" nation by not testing *for the moment*. The problem with this approach is that if a nation with thousands of nuclear weapons, capable of delivering them virtually anywhere on earth, is not willing to swear off nuclear testing in a legally binding fashion, it will be that much harder to get nations that have not yet developed nuclear weapons to do so.

So, aside from these anecdotal preferences, what *was* the Bush foreign policy as articulated on the campaign trail? Given how little candidates say of substance about *anything* in modern campaigns, Bush actually gave a reasonably detailed outline of where he claimed he wanted to take U.S. foreign policy. That outline is quite different from where he *actually* ended up taking our foreign policy, and the differences have almost nothing to do with adjustments made in the light of the September 11 attacks.

The element of the Bush agenda that was red meat to his neo-conservative backers was his repeated worship at the altar of missile defense. Bush took every opportunity to reiterate his promise to develop and deploy a system that would defend U.S. territory, U.S. troops, and U.S. allies. Although he was vague as to the shape of the new system, it was clear that if he wanted it to serve these diverse purposes it would have to be far more ambitious than the system that the Clinton administration had been investigating, which was focused on developing a small number of land-based interceptors in Alaska, possibly followed up with a second set of interceptors in North Dakota. Near the end of his term, Clinton gave a speech at his alma mater, Georgetown, in which he indicated that the technology simply was not ready to move toward deployment at this time.

Bush made it clear in his campaign that he disagreed with Clinton's missile defense skepticism. Bush's advisers suggested that if elected, Bush would not limit the system to land-based options, but would move full speed ahead to develop interceptors based at sea, lasers based on aircraft, and perhaps lasers or rockets based in space as well. If Bush were to do all of those things, he would be moving back toward the kind of ambitious, multi-tiered system that Ronald Reagan had contemplated in the 1980s. Never mind that the nation had already spent nearly $100 billion on missile defense testing with more failures than successes, or that independent experts like the Union of Concerned Scientists, MIT physicist Theodore Postol, and former top Pentagon weapons tester Philip Coyle had all indicated that a usable missile defense system was many years and many billions of dollars from being a reality, if it was doable at all. The true believers in missile defense wanted to build something, and they felt that George W. Bush was the guy who was finally going to do it, and fulfill an important unfinished piece of the Reagan agenda in the process. Whether or not it worked, this was going to be a huge bonanza for defense contractors like Boeing, Raytheon, and Lockheed Martin, which is one of the reasons they gave so generously to Dubya during the 2000 campaign.

According to the Center for Responsive Politics, arms manufacturers gave $190,000 to the Bush 2000 campaign, more than four times as much as they gave to the Gore/Lieberman ticket.[3] The Carlyle Group, the high-powered defense/high tech investment firm that had Bush family friend extraordinaire James Baker as a senior partner and the candidate's dad on retainer, gave $427,000 in campaign donations during the 2000 election cycle, with a whopping 84 percent going to Republican candidates.[4] That made Carlyle one of the most partisan campaign contributors in the entire 2000 election cycle. They clearly wanted a Republican in the White House, with a Republican Congress to rubber stamp his every decision. And they got their wish.

In addition to giving money to the Bush campaign, arms industry executives gave their time. Lockheed Martin vice president Bruce Jackson served as a finance chair for the Bush campaign and he would brag to his colleagues in the business about his role as chair of the Republican foreign policy platform committee. Jackson is a one-man military-industrial-complex. He has served as director of the U.S. Committee to Expand NATO during the run-up to the 1998 U.S. Senate vote to ratify the inclusion of Poland, Hungary, and the Czech Republic in the alliance. He has also served on the boards of the Project for the New American Century, a neo-con "dream team" that was founded with the backing of such Bush administration luminaries as Donald Rumsfeld, Paul Wolfowitz, Richard Perle, and Elliot Abrams, and of the Center for Security Policy, the pro-missile defense advocacy organization run by the ubiquitous gadfly, Frank Gaffney.[5]

Some of Bush's defense ideas were less than ideal from the point of view of his arms industry backers. Alongside his knee-jerk ideological support for missile defense, he also endorsed defense reform: a military that was characterized more by stealth, agility and quickness than it was by size. He wanted to procure fewer heavy tanks, fewer big attack submarines and lumbering aircraft carrier task forces—Cold War weapons designed to go up against the heavy metal of the Soviet armed forces—in favor of long-range strike systems, precision munitions, superior communications and targeting devices, and better trained forces who could capitalize on the information revolution to beat their adversaries through greater "situational awareness" on the battlefield. This part of the Bush agenda was not necessarily such good news for the big contractors. It could imply cutting cash cows that were bringing in billions of dollars now—the M-1 tank, the Crusader artillery system, one or more of the three new fighter planes in the pipeline, some heavy combat ships, some attack submarines—to make room for the more nimble weapons of the future, including sleeker, more mobile ships, smaller armored vehicles that would be easier to transport to distant battlefields, Unmanned Aerial Vehicles that could do surveillance in dangerous combat zones without risking the life of a pilot, and so forth. It's true, the same companies *losing* the contracts for the big Cold War relics would probably *gain* contracts by making the new stuff, but there could be delays in cash flow, and there could be a different distribution of contracts, and different states, localities, and congressional districts might benefit.

This type of defense reform would run up against entrenched interests in the military services, the arms contractors, and the Congress—folks who like their gravy trains to run on time, and didn't want to change *anything* if it meant cutting payrolls in their districts, or profits to their favorite company, or contributions to their favorite member of Congress. So, Bush's reform agenda, as articulated in the campaign, was definitely "against type," as they might say in

Hollywood. He was proposing ideas that, if carried out faithfully, might harm one of his key constituencies, at least in the short-term.

Bush's nuclear policy was a brilliantly crafted piece of propaganda that drew heavily on ideas developed by Stephen Hadley and others at conservative think tanks like the National Institute for Public Policy. Bush stressed the idea of unilateral nuclear arms reductions to levels below those previously contemplated by the Clinton/Gore administration, perhaps to as low as 1,500 to 2,000 deployed long-range nuclear bombs from then current levels of 6,500 to 7,500. This was a bold stroke, and even the arms control community, which had serious issues with Bush's general anti-treaty stance, had to sit up and take notice.

But Bush's proposed nuclear reductions turned out to be the bait in an elaborate bait-and-switch maneuver. Along with the reductions, which the United States would make unilaterally, and could reverse whenever Washington saw fit, would come the following: 1) Abandonment of the long-standing U.S. commitment to attempt to achieve congressional ratification of the Comprehensive Test Ban treaty; 2) Pursuit of a full-fledged, multi-tiered missile defense system; 3) A multi-billion dollar modernization of the U.S. nuclear weapons production and testing complex, including steps toward development of new, low-yield "mini-nukes." Under the guise of nuclear reductions, the Bush nuclear doctrine was a plan to upgrade the U.S. nuclear arsenal and re-start the nuclear arms race. But as with the other elements of his strategy, this was not so clear on the basis of a speech and a few references on the campaign trail. What *was* clear was that Bush seemed to be calling for deeper reductions in nuclear weapons than his Democratic rival, and that he had a novel and thoughtful nuclear plan.

Perhaps the most amazing thing about the Bush foreign policy doctrine as portrayed on the campaign trail was the fact that, thanks to Al Gore, Bush was allowed to give the impression that he was planning to spend less on the military than his Democratic rival. Gore and Lieberman routinely spoke of adding $100 billion to the Pentagon budget over ten years, a modest $10 billion per year increase to a budget that was approaching $300 billion per year. The Bush/Cheney ticket spoke about $50 billion in increases over a decade's time. However, the $50 billion referred to specific projects they were committed to funding, such as a special R&D fund for new high-tech weapons. It could not *possibly* have referred to their entire proposed increase over ten years, since their multi-tiered missile defense system alone would likely run $100 to $200 billion even without all the bells and whistles.

During many of the debates between Gore and Bush, Gore can be seen bragging about how he's planning to spend *more* on defense than George W. Bush is. *And Bush never disagrees with him.* In fact, in one of the debates, Bush makes the following statement: "If this is a race to see who can spend the most money, I'm going to lose." While Al Gore was going on about "new Marshall Plans" and other expensive-sounding foreign schemes, Bush described

America as a "humble nation," a nation that didn't assume it could go around remaking other countries in its image.

The first clue that this was not going to be a "kinder, humbler" brand of conservative foreign policy should have been when Bush chose his running mate, Dick Cheney.

— Chapter 1 Notes —

[1] Terry Neal, "Bush Falters in Foreign Policy Quiz: Asked by TV Reporter to Name Leaders, Connects on 1 of 4," *Washington Post*, November 5, 1999.

[2] "Mr. Bush's Exam," *Washington Post*, November 7, 1999.

[3] Cited in Dan Briody, *The Iron Triangle: Inside the Secret World of the Carlyle Group* (John Wiley and Sons, 2003), p. 92.

[4] Briody, op. cit., p. 92.

[5] For more on Jackson, see William D. Hartung and Michelle Ciarrocca, *Tangled Web: The Marketing of Missile Defense 1994-2000*, New York, World Policy Institute, June 2000; and William D. Hartung *Welfare for Weapons Dealers 1998: The Hidden Costs of NATO Expansion*, New York, World Policy Institute, 1998, available on the web at *www.worldpolicy.org/projects/arms*.

Dick Cheney and the
Power of the Self-Licking Ice Cream Cone

IN THE SUMMER of 2003, Chuck Spinney, a professional gadfly and true American patriot who has spent thirty years exposing waste, fraud, and abuse while working as a program analyst at the Pentagon, retired. To mark the occasion, Bill Moyers had Spinney on his PBS program *NOW with Bill Moyers*, to provide his distilled wisdom from thirty years of fighting the good fight, trying to rein in the military-industrial complex. One term leapt off the TV screen that evening. When Moyers asked about the skyrocketing salaries of military industry CEOs, Spinney described the concept of the "self-licking ice cream cone."

MOYERS: Have you seen these figures that CEO pay at Lockheed Martin went up from $5.8 million in 2000 to $25.3 million in 2002 . . . CEO pay went up at General Dynamics from $5.7 million in 2001 to $15.2 million in 2002. It went up at Honeywell from $12.9 million in 2000 to $45 million in 2002. . . . What do those figures say to you?

SPINNEY: Well, that's Versailles on the Potomac in action. It doesn't surprise me. The Defense Department, if you think about it, we really operate essentially according to an internal political economy. It's this closed cell that I mentioned earlier. In this bubble that developed during the Cold War . . .

The military-industrial complex is a political economy with a big P and a little E. It's very political in nature. Economic decisions, which should prevail in a normal market system, don't prevail in the Pentagon, or in the military-industrial complex.

So what we have is a system that essentially rewards its senior players. It's a self . . . what we call it, we have a term for it, it's a self-licking ice cream cone. We basically take care of ourselves. And that's why we have the metaphor that it's Versailles on the Potomac. It is basically self-referencing."[1]

The "self-licking ice cream cone" was a term that Spinney and his fellow critics of Pentagon waste had coined to describe not only the lavish pay schemes of military industry CEOs, but all the other sneaky ways in which weapons contractors, members of key congressional committees, Pentagon bureaucrats, and key decision makers in the White House and the military services conspire to throw money at weapons programs that may or may not be needed to defend the country, but which certainly *are* needed to keep the jobs, contracts, and campaign contributions flowing in key states and districts in what has become a virtual political protection racket. The political engineering that goes into weapons contracting, and the movement of top management personnel back and forth between positions in government and industry as part of the infamous "revolving door" syndrome, has created a situation in which high military budgets, exaggerated or distorted estimates of foreign threats, and overpriced, under-performing weapons systems have become the rule rather than the exception.

"Spending more in order to spend more" is the order of the day for these "beltway bandits." There is only one small problem with the system: Taxpayers are getting ripped off. Our defense priorities are being skewed toward Cold War relics that aren't of much use in dealing with the actual threats we now face, and the domestic side of the budget is getting the short end of the stick while most of our money goes to tax cuts for the well-to-do or to buy more $1-billion aircraft carriers and $200 million fighter planes that we don't need, and eventually won't be able to afford.

There is nothing new about these Pentagon spending practices. They have persisted and been nurtured by administrations of both parties ever since President Eisenhower gave his warning about the dangers of the military-industrial complex more than four decades ago. But they have reached their apogee under George W. Bush. And no one person better exemplifies just how far over the line we have gone toward a system that rewards individuals and corporations for who they know rather than what they know, and a system in which cronyism is more important than competence, than our current vice president, Dick Cheney.

Of all the loyal, secretive, inside-dealing cronies in the Bush camp, Cheney is the unrivalled master of the game. He is like the guy at the poker game who never makes a joke, never brags about his hand, but always seems to go home with the big pot of money at the end of the night while everyone else wonders what hit them.

You can say a lot of things about Dick Cheney, but nobody has ever accused him of being charismatic. He first burst into the national consciousness as part of the team that led the United States to victory in the 1991 Persian Gulf War, alongside Generals Colin Powell and Norman Schwarzkopf. During the Gulf War briefings Cheney was calm, precise, reassuring, authoritative, and boring to a fault. He couldn't match the animation, the good looks, the height, the uniforms, or the star power of his military colleagues.

After the war it was Powell and Schwarzkopf who signed the multi-million dollar book deals and bagged the major prime time television interviews, while Cheney faded from view. After a year or two out of the spotlight, deciding whether to launch his own campaign for the presidency,

Cheney finally got down to the business of earning his post-Gulf War bonanza. And he did it the old-fashioned way.

In time-honored Washington tradition, Cheney parlayed his experience in government into a job in one of the industries that he used to regulate. His move to Halliburton, an oil services and military construction firm with interests in virtually every corner of the globe, may end up being remembered as one of the most conflict-laden maneuvers in the history of the military-industrial complex.

Although he had no prior experience as a businessman, Cheney's name was thrown into the hopper as a possible CEO at Halliburton after one of his friends arranged for him to go on a fly-fishing trip with the company's then-chairman, Thomas Cruikshank, who was duly impressed with the former defense secretary. Since the company had a large share of its business in Middle Eastern oil producing states where Cheney was well known, have acting as George Bush's defense secretary in the 1991 gulf war, Halliburton sought Cheney not so much for his business acumen per se, but to serve as a "globetrotting rainmaker."[2]

Cheney's work as chief operating officer of Halliburtion, a Houston-based defense and oil-services firm, and his continuing relationship with the company, offers a unique window into the new brand of crony capitalism that is being forged under the leadership of Bush.

The revolving door between the government and weapons contractors isn't new, but it has reached new heights (monetarily) and depths (ethically), in recent years. Cheney's relationship with Halliburton is a perfect case study of all that is wrong with the relationship between our democratic form of government and the corporations that finance our elections and feed at the government trough on a daily basis.

Halliburton has its roots in two companies that were founded in the Texas/Oklahoma "oil patch" shortly after the end of World War I—Halliburton itself, an oil services firm founded by an Oklahoma entrepreneur named Erle Halliburton, and Brown and Root, a politically-wired construction firm which hitched its future to a young Texas congressman named Lyndon Baines Johnson in the late 1930s and early 1940s and never looked back. The two firms merged in 1963 under the name Halliburton, but maintained separate niches within a loose corporate structure until the late 1970s and early 1980s, when the U.S. recession and fluctuations in oil prices forced the managers of the company to more fully merge their disparate operations into one large streamlined firm with one hundred thousand employees operating in one hundred countries worldwide.[3]

Brown and Root's long and profitable relationship with Lyndon Johnson began when he secured a dam project for the company at a critical point in its early history. Many Pentagon contracts followed, including military construction work during the Vietnam War. Brown and Root and its principals did plenty to help LBJ's career along, including its fair share of bribes and questionable campaign contributions. It was a classic case of quid pro quo, Texas-style.

Dick Cheney's connection to the company, via his takeover of the top job at Halliburton in 1995, surpasses even LBJ for sheer conflicts-of-interest. As of this writing,

Cheney is still on Halliburton's payroll, receiving roughly $150,000 per year in deferred compensation while holding stock options on over 400,000 shares of the company. Halliburton recruited Cheney for his connections in the Middle East, and they paid off quite handsomely during his early years at the company. Not only did Halliburton's military contracting business increase dramatically as the firm started to supply military support services for U.S. "contingency operations" in Somalia, Rwanda, Haiti, Bosnia, and Kosovo, but U.S. government-guaranteed loans to the company jumped from roughly $100 million in the five years prior to Cheney's tenure as CEO to $1.5 billion in his five years at the helm. While Cheney attempted to avoid any obvious showboating related to the firm's growing military business—for example, he turned down several invitations from the U.S. Army to visit Halliburton's extensive Pentagon-financed operations in the Balkans—there is no question that his presence made it far easier for the company to cash in "big time," as he is fond of saying, on U.S. government contracts and guaranteed loans. As Halliburton vice president Bob Peebler put it, "Clearly Dick gave Halliburton some advantages. There's a lot of respect for Dick Cheney, both in the U.S. and around the world. From that perspective, doors would open."[4] Of course, the process wasn't as passive as Peebler made it sound—in order for the doors to open, Cheney had to come knocking, and he traveled the globe on Halliburton's behalf doing just that.

Halliburton's biggest "cash cow" during his tenure was definitely in the area of military support services, and the company's ability to earn so much in this area was directly tied to a decision Cheney had made back when he was secretary of defense in the first Bush administration. It was under Cheney's watch that the decision was made to privatize not only specific services in support of U.S. troops overseas—such as food services, or doing the laundry, or repairing vehicles—but to privatize the actual *planning process* that went into providing logistics for U.S. troops when they had to be sent into an inhospitable foreign hot spot on short notice.

In 1992, near the end of Cheney's tenure as defense secretary, Halliburton won a contract from the U.S. Army's Logistics Civil Augmentation Program (LOGCAP), which P.W. Singer has described as a deal to "work with the military in planning the logistical side of contingency operations." Singer notes that "it was the first time the U.S. military had ever contracted such global planning to a private organization."[5] In a pattern that would mark both Halliburton's and Cheney's business paths, the firm got the LOGCAP contract after conducting a top secret $3.9 million report for the Pentagon on how private companies could essentially provide the bulk of the logistics involved in major U.S. contingency deployments, from transportation and base-building to cooking the food and doing the laundry. The initial study contract called for a plan for how a private company could bear the bulk of the logistical burden for deploying 20,000 troops to 5 separate bases overseas within a 180-day period. Later in the year, Halliburton got a $5 million follow-on study contract to outline how a private firm might supply logistics for a series of more specific contingencies. By the end of the year, Halliburton had been selected to receive a five-year contract to be the U.S. Army's "on call" private logistics arm.[6]

The work started almost immediately. Halliburton was called upon to provide support services for U.S. forces deployed to Somalia as part of "Operation Restore Hope," an operation that began at the end of the Bush administration and carried over into the first Clinton term. As Singer notes, "Brown and Root employees arrived in Mogadishu just 24 hours after the first U.S. troops arrived and stayed until the final withdrawal in March 1995, when its employees left with the last U.S. marines." The company did everything from hiring local women to hand wash Army laundry to importing "a mortician to clean up the bodies of killed UN peacekeepers before shipping them out of the country."[7] Singer notes that for a good portion of its time in country, Halliburton was "the largest employer in Somalia, with some 2,500 local employees."[8]

The Somalia operation led to additional, more limited work on behalf of smaller U.S. deployments to Rwanda and Haiti. But the big payoff came in the Balkans, where Halliburton's Brown and Root Services unit started out supplying logistical support for Operation Deny Flight, the United Nations–mandated no-fly zone in Bosnia, and ended up building and operating bases and refugee camps in Croatia, Bosnia, and, most lucratively of all, in Kosovo. The firm's Balkan adventures started during the same year that Cheney took over as CEO of the company, and accounted for a good deal of the company's growth on the military side of its operations during his five-year tenure at the head of the firm.

The Army contract to provide logistical support for 20,000 U.S. troops deployed as part of the NATO IFOR forces in Bosnia came in at a cool $546 million, and it resulted in Halliburton doing work on behalf of U.S. and allied forces in Hungary, Bosnia, and Croatia. Just as it seemed that Halliburton had struck pure gold, there was a setback in 1997 when the company lost in its bid to renew its overall LOGCAP contract with the Army to a competitor, DynCorp, who had underbid them for the next round of work. But the sting was taken out of the loss when the Army decided to remove the Balkans work from the larger LOGCAP contract, allowing Halliburton to go full speed ahead on its lucrative support operations there.[9]

The Bosnia work set the stage for an even bigger role for Halliburton in Kosovo, where the company was involved in everything from building make-shift refugee quarters to building two major Army bases from scratch. The company's contract for its first year in Kosovo alone ballooned from the base level fee of $180 million to $1 billion. During its first three months in Kosovo alone, Singer reports that the company did the following: "built 192 barracks . . . thirteen helipads, two aviation-maintenance facilities, twelve mess-kitchen dining facilities, two large base dining facilities, and 37 temporary bathing facilities," even as it was delivering over 1 million meals, providing more than 55 million gallons of water, supplying over 383,000 gallons of diesel fuel, collecting over 89,000 cubic meters of trash, and loading and offloading over 4,200 containers with needed supplies.[10]

Halliburton's growth under Cheney's leadership is nothing compared to what it has done since he became vice president. In 2001, it won back the Army's LOGCAP contract, just in time to cash in on the logistical bonanza involved in providing facilities and provisions for U.S. troops in Afghanistan, Uzbekistan, Qatar, Kuwait, Iraq, and all the other far-flung outposts of the Bush administration's war on terrorism. The company is also in charge of making the cages used to house Taliban members and terror suspects at Guantánamo Bay, Cuba. A late August 2003 analysis in the *Washington Post* estimated that Halliburton had raked in $1.7 billion in military contracts in Iraq, Afghanistan, and beyond since the start of the Bush administration.[11]

The company's biggest prize—which it was awarded on a no-bid basis by the Army Corps of Engineers *after* Halliburton officials had helped the Defense Department write the specs for the contract—was an open-ended, two year contract worth up to $7 billion for putting out oil fires and repairing oil infrastructure in Iraq.

It was only after dogged questioning from Rep. Henry Waxman that it was revealed that the no-bid Halliburton contract was not merely for putting out oil fires, but for rebuilding and operating Iraq's extensive oil infrastructure.[12] Dan Baum revealed in his analysis of the deal in the *New York Times* magazine that Halliburton was uniquely situated to win the Iraqi oil industry rebuilding contract because the company actually *wrote* the contingency plan that the Army used to determine what work was needed. As Army spokesman Lt. Col. Gene Pawlik put it, "They were the company best positioned to execute the oil field work because of their involvement in the planning."[13] (This all sounds a bit like Dick Cheney's "self-selection" of himself to be Dubya's VP candidate, which will be discussed in a moment.)

Due to pressure by Waxman and other critics, the Pentagon finally agreed to re-bid the second phase of the Iraqi oil contract, to give other contractors a chance to work on the non-emergency elements of the job. But just one month after holding a major bidders' conference in Dallas to brief companies on the scope of work for the phase two Iraqi oil industry rebuilding contract, the Army Corps of Engineers accelerated the scheduled work so that the bulk of it would have to be done by Halliburton *before* a new contractor could take over. As a result of that administrative sleight of hand, what looked like a contract for $1 billion or more was cut back to a contract worth about $176 million.[14] Bechtel, itself a well-connected firm in Republican circles, cried foul and withdrew from the bidding. (When even an influential firm like Bechtel cries foul, you *know* the fix is in.)

Halliburton has been quick to show its gratitude to its Republican friends, earmarking 95 percent of its more than $708,000 in campaign donations from 1999 to 2002 to Republican candidates. And there's plenty more where that came from, heading straight for the Bush/Cheney 2004 campaign and the campaigns of their former CEO's Republican colleagues in the House and Senate.

Now that Bush's re-election bid is rolling in ill-gotten campaign cash from Halliburton and other companies tied to Cheney and other top officials in his administration, it's worth exploring a prior question. How did Dick Cheney become our vice president, arguably the most powerful vice president in recent memory? The similarities to Halliburton's self-dealing in awarding itself the contract to run Iraq's oil fields are striking.

During the 2000 presidential campaign, Cheney was supposed to be heading up the committee tasked with picking an appropriate running mate for George W. Bush. Given Bush's limited job experience, it was critical that the vice president be someone who could both serve as president if anything happened to George W. Bush, *and* help him "learn the ropes."

Phase one of selling young Dubya to the American people was "armoring" him on all sides with heavyweight advisors like Colin Powell, Condi Rice, George Shultz, and Paul Wolfowitz—the Vulcans. The vice-presidential selection had to build on this theme, and the choice of Cheney, a trusted Bush family advisor and former key cabinet member in his father's administration, was an indicator of just how seriously "Team Bush" was taking this decision.

In the months that followed, some of the names that turned up as possible running mates included Colin Powell, Pennsylvania Governor Tom Ridge, Oklahoma Governor Frank Keating, New York Governor George Pataki, Nebraska Senator Chuck Hagel, Tennessee Senator Bill Frist, former Missouri Senator John Danforth, and, briefly, vanquished

Bush rival Senator John McCain of Arizona. All the candidates being seriously considered were sent rigorous questionnaires—which included eighty-three questions on health, financial, and other sensitive personal and professional matters that were designed to help avoid unpleasant last minute surprises.

These were all serious men, all far more experienced in government than the nominee himself, but they were lacking in a few key areas that have proven to be key indicators of survival for members of team Dubya. Some—such as Powell and Pataki—were not conservative enough to satisfy Bush's neo-Reaganite, neo-conservative base. The other quality that is essential in a true George W. Bush functionary is deep and abiding loyalty to the president and his family.

After searching high and low over a three-month period, Cheney came up with an unexpected choice. Much like little Jack Horner from the nursery rhyme, who stuck in his thumb, pulled out a plum, and said, "oh what a good boy am I!", Cheney surveyed the field and decided that there really was no candidate more qualified than the head of the selection committee, the long-time Bush family friend, his father's defense secretary in Gulf War I, the man himself,—the envelope please—and the vice-presidential nomination goes to—Dick Cheney!

As George W. Bush explained it in his speech formally announcing the selection of Cheney, it sounded almost like a platonic relationship that had blossomed in spring into a full-blown romance: "For months we worked closely together to review the qualifications of many impressive candidates.

As we worked to evaluate the strength of others I saw first-hand Dick Cheney's outstanding judgment. . . . And gradually I realized that the person who was best qualified to be my vice-presidential nominee was working by my side."[15]

Bush had asked Cheney at the beginning of the selection process if he was interested in the VP slot and Dick said no, but according to Bush "I kept the thought of him joining me in the back of my mind."[16] This raises the question of whether the selection process was in whole or in part a charade, just another attempt for Bush to demonstrate his commitment to "compassionate conservatism," "diversity," and a big tent for the Republican Party by considering folks like Colin Powell and George Pataki publicly, while privately knowing at a certain point that the fix was in for Uncle Dick.

In an analysis piece that ran shortly after Cheney was selected, Adam Nagourney and Frank Bruni of the *New York Times* noted that "Cheney's own candidacy was moving along a track so secret that some of the other politicians on the list of seemingly serious prospects had no idea that Mr. Bush was settling on him until they learned it from newspaper and television reports about 72 hours before Mr. Bush formally announced the decision."[17]

Although no one could question Cheney's credentials—White House chief of staff under Gerald Ford, house minority whip during a ten year stint as a representative from the state of Wyoming, secretary of defense under Bush the elder in the Gulf War—some of the Republican faithful *were* fit to be tied about the *process* through which Cheney was selected. The Gore campaign gleefully jumped on Cheney's conservative votes in Congress, his close ties to Bush's father, and his recent history as CEO of a major oil services firm to suggest that his selection marked a long step back from Bush's avowed "compassionate conservatism" to a Neanderthal brand of Republicanism.[18] It didn't help matters that the Bush campaign's attempts to explain exactly how Cheney, who was running the selection process, could have undergone comparable scrutiny to the folks he was interviewing and sending eighty-three-question surveys to, bordered on the comical. Bush campaign spokesperson Karen Hughes simply said "Secretary Cheney told me he subjected himself to the same kind of scrutiny," as the other candidates. Eyebrows were raised further when one potential VP candidate noted that some of the materials he received came in an envelope from the law offices of Cheney's daughter Elizabeth, suggesting that she too had been involved in the VP screening process. When asked whether she might have been involved in vetting her own father, Hughes refused to answer, saying "I am not able to discuss others who were involved in the screening process" other than Cheney, candidate Bush, and Bush campaign manager Joe Allbaugh.[19]

On the issue of how Cheney's politics might play in the campaign, Alison Mitchell of the *New York Times* may have put it best, albeit in understated tones, when she noted that, "The difficulty for Mr. Bush is that some of the stands of his running mate cut right to the heart of the way he has been seeking to define himself as a 'compassionate conservative'."[20] Maureen Dowd was less polite, noting that given the Republican convention's opening theme of "leave no child behind" (a slogan the Bush campaign stole lock, stock, and barrel from the liberal Children's Defense Fund, an organization that Hillary Rodham Clinton served on the board of for many years), "it will be delicious to see how the Republicans deal with those Cheney votes against Head Start." Dowd also reminded her readers that "in Congress, Mr. Cheney was way, way out there, always willing to pony up money to guerillas in Nicaragua and Angola but not to poor women whose lives were endangered by pregnancies." She further observed that " 'Inclusive' loses a little punch when you are running with someone who in 1986 opposed a call to release Nelson Mandela after 23 years in prison, and often voted against economic sanctions that helped crush apartheid."[21]

His consistently right-wing ideology is the key to understanding Cheney, but eventually it all comes back to the money. In an article entitled "Cheney As Vice President Faces Serious Cut in Pay," Gary Strauss of USA Today noted that Cheney's salary of $181,400 plus expenses for serving as vice president would be a tiny fraction of the $26.4 million compensation package he earned in his last year as CEO of Halliburton, not to mention holdings of Halliburton stock worth an additional $46 million. And Lynne Cheney was no slouch either, earning $300,000 in "retainers and stock compensation as a director at defense contractor Lockheed Martin, publisher Reader's Digest Association, energy services firm Union Pacific Resources Group, and Amex/IDS, the mutual fund arm of the financial services behemoth

American Express." Lynne Cheney's Lockheed Martin compensation alone clocked in at $120,000, and together with
her husband's millions from Halliburton put the Cheney
family deeply in debt to the military-industrial sector for a
substantial portion of their very prosperous livelihoods.[22]

How Cheney became Bush's vice president, and how
Halliburton received a favored position in post-war Iraq, are
part and parcel of a larger set of issues. Will the American
public continue to sit still for Bush and Cheney's blatant
conflicts of interest? Issuing no-bid contracts to companies
with financial and professional ties to its own top officials
is business as usual in the administration of George W.
Bush, but in the case of Halliburton the symbolism and
reality of filling the coffers of the vice president's former
firm—a company that is still writing checks to him as part
of his golden parachute that was negotiated when he left to
join the Bush campaign—is particularly egregious.

Meanwhile, Cheney is in deep denial regarding his
Halliburton connection. In a mid-September appearance
on NBC's *Meet the Press*, Cheney asserted that he had "sev-
ered all my ties to the company, gotten rid of all my financial interests. I have no financial interest in Halliburton of
any kind and haven't had now for over three years."
Cheney's claim drove senate majority leader Tom Daschle
to argue that the vice president "needs to explain how he
reconciles the claim that he has 'no financial interest of any
kind' with the hundreds of thousands of dollars in deferred
salary payments he receives from Halliburton." In shades of
Bill Clinton's verbal gymnastics over "what the meaning of

'is' is" in his explanations of the Monica Lewinsky affair, Cheney's spokesperson Catherine Martin asserted that his deferred payments—which clocked in at a hefty $162,393 in 2002—are "not a tie" to Halliburton. [23]

If Congress isn't ready to launch a war profiteering probe, then citizen's groups should start demanding one. The pension funds of the New York City cops and fire-fighters have filed suit against Halliburton to find out why their subsidiary's business dealings in Iran do not constitute trading with an adversary, an offense which should in theory disqualify the company from receiving Pentagon contracts of any kind. The deeper one digs into the actions of Cheney and his former company, the more questions come up. The time to get answers to these questions is now, before the Bush/Cheney ticket stands for re-election. And given their record of stonewalling and distortion, it would make sense to get the answers under oath, either in a duly constituted congressional investigation or in a court of law.

— Chapter 2 Notes —

[1] "Transcript—Bill Moyers Interviews Chuck Spinney," based on Spinney's appearance on "Now with Bill Moyers, " August 1, 2003. The transcript is available at *www.pbs.org*, by clicking on "Now With Bill Moyers" and going to the show for that date. Moyers' data on defense CEO pay are from Chris Hartman and David Martin, "More Buck for the Bang: CEO Pay at Top Defense Contractors," United for a Fair Economy, April 28, 2003.

[2] Leslie Wayne, Richard A. Oppel, and James Risen, "Gulf War Led Cheney to the Board Room," *New York Times* July 27, 2000.

[3] For a good, brief capsule history of Halliburton see P.W. Singer, *Corporate Warriors: The Rise of the Privatized Military Industry* (Ithaca, New York: Cornell University Press, 2003), Chapter 9, pp., 136–148.

[4] P.W. Singer, op. cit., p. 140.

[5] Singer, *Corporate Warriors*, op. cit., p. 138.

[6] Singer, "Corporate Warriors," pp. 142–143.

[7] Singer, op. cit., p. 143.

[8] Ibid., p. 143.

[9] Singer, op. cit., pp. 144–145.

[10] Singer, op. cit., p. 145—his source is an article by Donald T. Wynn, "Managing the Logistics-Support Contract in the Balkans Theater," in *Engineer* magazine, July 2000, available on the army's web site at *http://call.army.mil/call/trngqtr/tq4-00/wynn.htm*.

[11] Michael Dobbs, "Halliburton's Deals Greater Than Thought," *Washington Post*, August 29, 2003.

[12] To see Waxman's highly informative series of exchanges with the Army Corps of Engineers on Halliburton's role in Iraq, see the web site of the House Committee on Government Reform, at *www.house.gov/reform,* and click on the section for the minority caucus.

[13] Dan Baum, "Nation Builders for Hire," *New York Times Magazine,* June 22, 2003.

[14] Neela Bannerjee, "Bechtel Ends Move for Work in Iraq, Seeing a Done Deal," *New York Times*, August 8, 2003.

15 "The 2000 Campaign: The Choice for a Running Mate; Excerpts From Statements by Bush and His Running Mate," *New York Times*, July 26, 2000.

16 'Excerpts," op. cit., note 5.

17 For the best synopsis of Bush and Cheney's VP "self-selection" process and its peculiarities, see Adam Nagourney and Frank Bruni, "Gatekeeper to Running Mate: Cheney's Road to the Candidacy," *New York Times*, July 28, 2000.

18 The quote is from Nagourney and Bruni, op. cit. above.

19 Nagourney and Bruni, "Gatekeeper to Running Mate," op. cit.

20 Alison Mitchell, "The 2000 Campaign: Running Mate—Once Again, Cheney Confronts Questions," July 28, 2000.

21 Maureen Dowd, "A Babysitter for Junior," *New York Times*, July 26, 2000.

22 Gary Strauss, "Cheney As Vice President Faces a Serious Cut in Pay," *USA Today*, July 26, 2000.

23 Mike Allen and Dana Milbank, "Aides Back Cheney on Lack of Halliburton Ties," *Washington Post*, September 17, 2003.

3

Donald Rumsfeld and the Princes of Darkness

"You get a lot more with a kind word and a gun than you do with a kind word alone."

—DONALD RUMSFELD, quoting fellow Chicagoan Al Capone at the Center for Security Policy's "Keeper of the Flame" awards, October 7, 1998

"As through this world I ramble, I've seen lots of funny men. Some will rob you with a six gun, and some with a fountain pen."

—WOODY GUTHRIE, "Pretty Boy Floyd"

 **DONALD RUMSFELD IS** a smart, tough, totally focused individual with a better than average sense of humor. He's motivated more by ideas than by money. In many respects he is a highly capable person, but unfortunately, Rumsfeld is drunk on ideology. His intelligence, wit, and managerial skill are all narrowly focused on the promotion of a Hobbesian world view, one in which the guy with the most guns—and the willingness to use them—is the one who prevails.

Just as John Ashcroft's crusade against the Bill of Rights has undermined our democracy at home, Rumsfeld's arrogant posturing has undercut our position abroad, and alienated long-standing allies like France and Germany.

If his selection of Dick Cheney as his running mate was the first sign that George W. Bush's "compassionate conservative" approach to foreign policy was lurching sharply to the right, his choice of Donald Rumsfeld as his secretary of defense sealed the deal.

Rumsfeld's profile is remarkably similar that of his old friend Dick Cheney: a former White House chief of staff, a former secretary of defense, a former member of Congress, and a former CEO of a major corporation (in Rumsfeld's case, several major corporations). As a Republican congressman from a Chicago-area district in the 1960s, Rumsfeld had voted for civil rights legislation before going on to work at the Office of Economic Opportunity under Richard Nixon. This seemingly moderate profile offered a sharp contrast to Cheney's ultra-conservative voting record in his stint as a congressman from Wyoming. As for his business career, Rumsfeld's service as CEO at the pharmaceutical firm G. D. Searle, the high-tech giant General Instruments, and the bio-tech firm Gilead Sciences suggested a broader background than Cheney's service at Halliburton. Rumsfeld's résumé, combined with his ability to sound calm and rational even while mouthing rabid right-wing propaganda, probably explains why he didn't get more flak from Congress or the press before taking charge at the Pentagon.

During his first stint as secretary of defense during Gerald Ford's presidency, Rumsfeld occupied the far right wing of that administration. While Ford's secretary of state Henry Kissinger was flying off to Moscow to promote the SALT II Strategic Arms Limitation Treaty, Rumsfeld was in Washington, whispering exaggerated versions of the Soviet threat into Ford's ear and siding with neo-conservatives on Capitol Hill who were trying to strangle the treaty in its infancy.

As Ford's secretary of defense, Rumsfeld was a mouth-piece for the views of his neo-con counterparts in the Committee on the Present Danger (CPD), a right-wing propaganda outfit spearheaded by hard-line anti-Soviet intellectuals like Eugene Rostow and Norman Podhoretz, and supported by prominent Republican conservatives like George Shultz and Ronald Reagan.[1] The CPD, which followed in the intellectual footsteps of University of Chicago political scientist Albert Wohlstetter and the political footsteps of Sen. Henry "Scoop" Jackson (D-WA), claimed that the CIA's professional analysts were drastically understating the extent of Soviet military power.

To placate the CPD and its conservative brethren, the Ford administration agreed to appoint a panel known as "Team B." The members reviewed the CIA's intelligence on the Soviet threat and came to their own conclusions. Given their ideological slant, they argued that the Soviet Union was far more dangerous than we had ever imagined, and that the CIA, then under the direction of George Herbert Walker Bush—was "soft" on the Soviet threat. Rumsfeld openly embraced the panel's findings, using them as ammunition to undermine the SALT II Treaty.

Given his continuing penchant for exaggeration in the service of his political goals, it may be of interest to know that Rumsfeld's hyped view of the mid-1970s Soviet threat was wildly off the mark.[2] When the Soviet Union collapsed and the KGB archives were opened, it became clear that if anything the CIA's mid-1970s analysis of Soviet capabilities were an overstatement. In other words, the Team B report was an exaggeration of an overstatement, signifying nothing—other than the fact that neo-conservative fantasies die hard.

When it further emerged that U.S. assessments of specific Soviet weapons initiatives had been exaggerated by double agents like the CIA's Aldrich Ames, one would have thought that somewhere there would be a neo-con who would admit that their exaggerated views of the Soviet menace drove this country to waste hundreds of billions—if not trillions—of tax dollars, all in the name of a threat that never existed on the scale suggested by the prophets of gloom and doom at the CPD.

There may be a few minor figures in the neo-con pantheon who have admitted their past misjudgments, but Donald Rumsfeld isn't one of them. He still maintains the same rigid, Manichean worldview that he held in the 1970s. For Rumsfeld, only the names of the enemies have changed.

Rumsfeld and his allies still cling to the "Team B"-style tactic of using handpicked panels dominated by their neo-con friends to exaggerate the threats to the United States, all under the guise of conducting an objective "second look" at U.S. intelligence. It worked in the 1970s when the subject was the Soviet threat, and it worked in the late 1990s when Rumsfeld chaired a panel tasked with assessing the Third World ballistic missile threat. Sadly, it also worked in 2002, when Rumsfeld and his cronies used an exaggerated view of Saddam Hussein's nuclear, chemical, and biological weapons capabilities to spur the rush to war with Iraq.

While George Herbert Walker Bush was busy trying to get the CIA back in line with basic notions of competence after revelations of the agency's illegal covert activities, Secretary of Defense Rumsfeld was building his reputation and alliances, placing his 34-year-old protégé Dick Cheney in his former job as White House Chief of staff.[3] But Rumsfeld's ultimate dream of succeeding his boss Gerald Ford as president was a non-starter. Ronald Reagan was the darling of the ascendant neo-conservative movement, while Rumsfeld was a bit player by comparison.

With no hope of landing the top job in the government, Rumsfeld left the public sector behind for a successful career in business, where he maintained his staunch right-wing views and kept his eye out for opportunities to shape government policy. And there were many uses for a man of his stature in promoting Republican policies of the 1980s and 1990s. On November 3, 1983, Reagan appointed Rumsfeld, who was then an executive at the G.D. Searle pharmaceutical company, to take up the position of Mideast special envoy, which was being vacated by Robert "Bud" MacFarlane. During his tenure in the position, which lasted through May 18, 1984, Rumsfeld was involved in complex issues relating to the U.S. military presence in Lebanon and the Israeli-Palestinian conflict.[4] He was also in charge of outreach to Saddam Hussein's regime in Iraq. Rumsfeld's mission in Iraq was to attempt to foster a warming of relations with Baghdad so that Washington could build up Hussein's regime as a bulwark against Iran, which was viewed as a greater potential danger to U.S. interests in the region.

On December 20, 1883, Rumsfeld held a lengthy face-to-face meeting with Saddam Hussein and his chief foreign policy operative Tariq Aziz. Their relationship blossomed into a covert U.S.-Iraqi alliance, in which Washington provided military technology and tactical intelligence to the Iraqi military in an effort to strengthen its ability to hold off, and hopefully defeat, the numerically superior Iranian forces. The Reagan administration's attitude toward Iraqi chemical weapon usage was surprisingly relaxed during this period. Baghdad had begun its use of chemical weapons against Iranian forces before Rumsfeld took up his post as special envoy. On November 1, 1983, State Department official Jonathan Howe sent a memo to Secretary of State George Shultz reporting "almost daily use of CW [chemical weapons]" by Iraq against Iranian forces.[5] By March 26, 1984, when Rumsfeld held a follow-up meeting in Baghdad with Tariq Aziz, a United Nations investigation had confirmed that Iraq had been using chemical munitions against Iranian forces.[6] Although Rumsfeld and other Reagan officials expressed private displeasure at these attacks, no public condemnation was issued. These same chemical weapons attacks were cited nearly two decades later by Secretary of

Defense Rumsfeld and George W. Bush as rhetorical ammunition in their case for overthrowing Hussein's regime.

Ask Reagan administration alumni about their administration's cozy stance toward Saddam Hussein's regime during
the 1980s, and they will assure you that they "protested" his
use of chemical weaponry. This is a blatant rewriting of history. Whatever discouraging words Reagan administration
officials may have uttered to Saddam or his henchman
clearly rang hollow in comparison to the increases in U.S.
technology transfers and tactical intelligence that flowed to
Iraq in the years after Rumsfeld broke the ice with Saddam.
Between 1985 and 1990, the years between Rumsfeld's
tenure as special envoy and the first Persian Gulf War, the
United States government licensed the export of $1.5 billion
worth of militarily useful equipment from U.S. companies
to Iraq. Before sanctions were imposed on Iraq in connection with its August 2, 1990 invasion of Kuwait, $500 mil-
lion of that equipment had already made its way into
Hussein's military machine, including anthrax, bubonic
plague, and other precursors for chemical and biological
weapons. There were parts destined for the Iraqi Atomic
Energy Agency, a key player in Hussein's nuclear weapons
program; and machinery for use at the Saad 16 missile production complex south of Baghdad. During this same period, the Reagan and George H.W. Bush State Departments
also signed off on a number of third party transfers of U.S.-
origin equipment to Iraq, including U.S.-designed howitzers
from Austria and U.S.-manufactured components that
ended up in cluster bombs that Chilean arms dealers Carlos

Cardoen sold to Hussein's military forces. An account by Michael Dobbs of the *Washington Post* suggests that CIA Director William Casey may have played an active role in soliciting third-party suppliers like Cardoen to supply weaponry to Baghdad as part of Washington's "tilt" toward Iraq.[7]

The United States also stepped up its provision of tactical intelligence to Iraq, intelligence that helped Hussein's forces target Iranian forces with both chemical and conventional bombs. Far from holding back when the full horrors of Iraqi weapons use against Iranian military personnel and Kurdish civilians became known, the Reagan administration actually *increased* intelligence-sharing with Baghdad during 1988, the year of Iraq's massive chemical attacks on Halabja and other Kurdish towns in Northern Iraq.[8]

Rumsfeld also made an explicit pitch to Saddam for the construction of an Iraqi oil pipeline that would run through Jordan to the Red Sea port of Aqaba. In notes on his December 1983 meeting with Tariq Aziz, Rumsfeld reported: "I noted that Iraq's oil exports were important . . . I raised the question of a pipeline through Jordan. He said he was familiar with the proposal. It apparently was a U.S. company's proposal."[9] The pipeline project was the brainchild of Secretary of State Shultz's former company, Bechtel—the same company that is now cashing in on the Pentagon's privatized occupation of Iraq.

While Rumsfeld has downplayed his role in opening the door to the de facto U.S. alliance with Saddam Hussein, he is proud of his other two major forays into advising the U.S.

government: his chairmanships of the 1998 Commission to Assess the Ballistic Missile Threat to the United States and a 2001 blue ribbon panel on national security missions in space.

The ballistic missile panel—commonly referred to as the Rumsfeld commission—was promoted by the Center for Security Policy (CSP), a right-wing think tank founded by Frank Gaffney. Gaffney started CSP in 1988, shortly after he left the Reagan administration over his disapproval of two major nuclear arms control initiatives, the Intermediate Nuclear Forces (INF) agreement and the Strategic Arms Reduction Treaty (START). Gaffney and his network never fully accepted Reagan's evolution from describing the Soviet Union as an "evil empire" in his first term to becoming a staunch advocate of deep nuclear reductions in his second term. Gaffney founded his think tank with support from right-wing stalwarts including Richard Mellon Scaife and the Coors family—and weapons contractors like Martin Marietta, Lockheed, and Boeing.

From the early 1990s onward, Gaffney's center has served as the de facto nerve center of the Star Wars lobby. It was CSP board member Curt Weldon (R-PA) who inserted an amendment into the FY 1997 Pentagon authorization bill calling for a "Team B"-style second look at the U.S. intelligence community's assessment of the ballistic missile threat posed by so-called rogue nations like Iran, Iraq, and North Korea. The purpose of the exercise would be similar to that of the original "Team B" of the 1970s—to hype the threat posed by North Korea, an impoverished nation that spends—in a good year—less than 1 percent of what the United States devotes to its military forces.[10]

North Korea needed to be hyped as a viable threat because the missile defense issue had been losing steam on Capitol Hill. Gaffney had managed to convince Newt Gingrich and Dick Armey to make immediate deployment of a missile defense system a core demand in the "Contract With America," the platform that was used to fuel the Republican takeover of the House of Representatives in the 1994 midterm elections. But this process had been stalled when a Congressional Budget Office report had put the cost of deploying and maintaining a ground-based national missile defense system at up to $60 billion over several decades, a price tag that resulted in "sticker shock" even among some Gingrich camp followers on Capitol Hill.

Enter Donald Rumsfeld, to rescue the floundering missile defense program. The bulk of the membership of his nine-member panel consisted of pro-missile defense ideologues handpicked by House Speaker Newt Gingrich. From a public relations standpoint, Rumsfeld's approach was brilliant. He basically reframed the issue of the missile defense threat in the most pessimistic, worst-case perspective possible. Instead of worrying about a missile reaching the American heartland, what about a missile launched from North Korea that could reach the end of the Aleutian Island chain in Alaska? What if North Korea or another U.S. adversary was willing to develop a relatively crude missile without rigorous testing and launch it—or threaten to launch it—against a target in the United States? What if

China or some other allegedly friendly state was willing to sell North Korea a complete ballistic missile?

By redefining the missile threats, Rumsfeld was effectively able to exaggerate the danger that they posed. The panel's bottom line was that a determined nation might be able to develop a ballistic missile capable of reaching U.S. soil "within five years of the decision to do so," not the ten to fifteen years estimated by professional intelligence analysts in the U.S. government.

Newt Gingrich immediately started pushing the Rumsfeld panel's report as "the greatest warning for U.S. security since the end of the Cold War." Much of the mainstream media fell into step with Rumsfeld and Gingrich's alarmist rhetoric.

It was scare-mongering of the highest order, and it worked like a charm. When the North Korean regime made the serious blunder of firing a crude ballistic missile into the Pacific Ocean in the summer of 1998, the Star Warriors had all the ammunition they needed to push through a bill declaring that it would henceforth be the policy of the United States government to deploy a national missile defense system. The fact that North Korea had shown a willingness to negotiate away its nuclear weapons and ballistic missiles as part of the 1994 U.S.–North Korea framework agreement meant very little in the hyper-charged environment caused by the Rumsfeld panel report and the North Korean missile test. One of the few voices of sanity belonged to the U.S. government's top missile threat analyst, Robert Walpole, who had repeatedly argued in congressional testimony that a ballistic missile was the least likely vehicle a rogue state would choose to use in launching an attack against the United States, for the simple reason that it has a "return address" that would invite rapid and devastating retaliation.

For his loyal service to the missile defense cause, Rumsfeld was awarded the Center for Security Policy's "Keeper of the Flame Award" at its annual fundraising dinner on October 7, 1998. *New York Times* columnist William Safire served as the master of ceremonies, ushering Rumsfeld into the select circle of award recipients that had included Ronald Reagan, Newt Gingrich, and other right-wing luminaries. In the Center for Security Policy's 1998 annual report, Gaffney described Rumsfeld as an informal advisor and special friend of CSP; but he was also a donor, alongside major weapons makers like Lockheed Martin, Northrop Grumman, and Boeing. Gaffney's group has received over $2 million in corporate donations since its founding in 1988, and many of the tables at the 1998 gala were filled by weapons company representatives.

Since he received his "Keeper of the Flame" award in 1998, Rumsfeld has led the charge for the U.S. withdrawal from the anti-ballistic missile (ABM) treaty, and dramatically increased missile defense funding from $4 to $5 billion in the Clinton era to $10 billion per year and more during his tenure. He has persuaded President Bush to undertake a crash program to deploy some sort of missile defenses on land, at sea, and on airplanes, regardless of whether such a system actually works. And to make sure the public can't find out whether or not the system is workable, Rumsfeld has reduced the amount of information that the Pentagon's

Missile Defense Agency has to provide on the costs and performance of the costly missile defense components that it is funding.

As noted earlier, Rumsfeld also chaired a second panel, called the Commission to Assess United States National Security Space Management and Organization. The congressional sponsor of the amendment creating the panel was another member of the Center for Security Policy's advisory board, former New Hampshire senator Bob Smith. Rumsfeld has moved swiftly to implement the panel's findings, which include a plan to centralize U.S. procurement of military space assets in one place and to put the U.S. in a position to deploy weapons in space at some future date if the President chooses to do so. In May of 2001, Rumsfeld invited Bob Smith to speak at the Pentagon at the unveiling of his new plan for national security space activities. At the same ceremony, he announced the creation of a new assistant secretary's position in the Air Force that would be in charge of procuring everything from spy satellites to space-based elements of missile defense. Peter B. Teets was later chosen to fill that post. He is a former chief operating officer at Lockheed Martin, the nation's largest weapons contractor and a major player in the missile defense and military space fields.[11]

In November of 2001, Rumsfeld made a return appearance at the Center for Security Policy's "Keeper of the Flame" awards dinner, this time as a sitting secretary of defense. During his remarks, he turned to Gaffney and said, "Frank, if there ever was any doubt about the power of your ideas, one only has to look at the number of Center associates who people this administration . . . I was thinking of calling a staff meeting, but I think I'll wait until tomorrow morning."[12]

In all, Gaffney's group boasts twenty-two former advisors or board members in the Bush administration, from Undersecretary of Defense Douglas Feith—former chair of the CSP board—to Secretary of the Air Force James Roche, to Pentagon Comptroller Dov Zakheim, to former Defense Policy Board chairman (and continuing member) Richard Perle.[13] During the administrations of George Herbert Walker Bush and Bill Clinton, Gaffney and his band of right-wing ideologues were on the outside looking in. Under George W. Bush, the Star Wars lobby is running the show, and their favorite son, Donald Rumsfeld, is running the Department of Defense.

No treatment of Donald Rumsfeld would be complete without a brief look at his career as a businessman. As with all of Rumsfeld's activities, it has sometimes been difficult to tell where his political preferences ended and his business interests began. In the early 1990s, he was installed as CEO of the General Instruments Corporation by takeover specialist Ted Forstmann, a Rumsfeld political associate who helped found the neo-con advocacy group Empower America. Rumsfeld sat on Empower America's board prior to joining the Bush administration. Forstmann also placed Rumsfeld and his current Bush administration nemesis Colin Powell on the board of Gulfstream Aerospace when his firm acquired it during the 1990s merger boom.

Rumsfeld cashed out $11 million in gulfstream stock when the company was bought out by weapons maker General Dynamics in 1999.

Cashing in on his neo-con connections was far from the most controversial aspect of his business career. That honor is reserved for his stint on the board of ABB, a Zurich, Switzerland-based engineering firm that received a $200 million contract to provide two nuclear reactors to North Korea as part of the 1994 agreed framework accord between Washington and Pyongyang. While supporters of the deal have argued that the light-water reactors that ABB is building for North Korea are far more difficult to use for nuclear bomb-making than Pyongyang's current reactor designs, Rumsfeld's neo-con pals have kept up a steady stream of criticism of the deal. Rumsfeld's own 1998 panel on the third world ballistic threat accused Pyongyang of running a secret nuclear weapons program, a charge that one would have thought would make Rumsfeld sensitive to the implications of a nuclear reactor sale to the regime by a company he was associated with.

Rumsfeld has asserted that he knew nothing of the deal, which is extremely hard to believe given the fact that he was ABB's only American board member from 1990 to 2001, the period straddling the company's reactor sale to North Korea. Former ABB officials told *Fortune* magazine that the deal was discussed at several board meetings that he attended, and that all ABB board members would have received a written summary of the details on the contract to supply reactors to North Korea. ABB's CEO went to North Korea in November

1999 to hype the deal, which he described as a "wide-ranging, long-term cooperation agreement" with Pyongyang.[14] And, as *Newsweek* noted in a report on the controversy, "in the event Rumsfeld simply nodded off every time the topic came up, ABB celebrated the deal in a January 2000 press release headlined: "ABB to Deliver Systems, Equipment to North Korea Nuclear Plants. $200 million in orders awarded under multi-government framework agreement." Surely a board member totally uninterested in nukes—let alone Rumsfeld—would have read that."[15]

In a clear sign of the fear that Rumsfeld inspires both in and outside of the U.S. government, fourteen of the fifteen ABB board members who were involved with the company at the time of the North Korean reactor deal refused to speak on the record about it to *Fortune* magazine reporter Richard Behar. The fifteenth board member spoke only on condition that his name be withheld. Rumsfeld clearly doesn't want his North Korea connection to be revealed, but his silence may speak louder than words.

[1] For a history of the CPD and its successful campaign to undermine arms control treaties in the 1970's and beyond, see Anne Hessing Cahn, *Killing Détente: The Right Attacks the CIA* (Pennsylvania State University Press, 1998).

[2] In fact, there is strong evidence to suggest that the CIA estimate of Soviet military strength that Rumsfeld and his Team B buddies were ridiculing as being too low was in fact too high. See John Prados, *The Soviet Estimate: U.S. Intelligence Analysis and Russian Military Strength* (New York: Dial Press, 1982).

[3] For background on Rumsfeld's mid-1970's political maneuvers, see Mark Thompson and Michael Duffy, "Pentagon Warlord," *Time*, January 27, 2003.

[4] For background on Rumsfeld's service as Reagan's special envoy to the Middle East, see George Shultz, *Turmoil and Triumph: My Years as Secretary of State* (New York: Charles Scribner's and Sons, 1993), pp 228–229 and 435–439.

[5] Michael Dobbs, "U.S. Had Key Role in Iraq Buildup—Trade in Chemical Arms Allowed Despite Their Use on Iranians, Kurds," *Washington Post*, December 30, 2002.

[6] Jim Vallette, with Steve Kretzmann and Daphne Wysham, *Crude Visions: How Oil Interests Obscured U.S. Government Focus on Chemical Weapons Use by Saddam*, Washington, DC, Institute for Policy Studies, August 13, 2003, p. 6.

[7] Michael Dobbs, "U.S. Had Key Role in Iraq Buildup," op. cit. For a concise history of U.S. efforts to arm Iraq during the mid-1980's, see "Who Armed Iraq," in William D. Hartung, *And Weapons for All* (New York: Harper Collins, 1995), pp. 224–249.

[8] Michael Dobbs, "U.S. Had Key Role in Iraq Buildup," op. cit.

[9] The quote from Rumsfield's notes on his meeting with Aziz is from Jim Vallette, "Crude Vision," op. cit., p. 13, note 13.

[10] For more on Gaffney and CSP, see William D. Hartung and Michelle Ciarrocca, "Tangled Web: The Marketing of Missile Defense 1994–2000," New York, World Policy Institute, June 2000, pp. 6–8, and the CSP website, at *www.securitypolicy.org*. On the North Korean threat as of 2002, the International Institute for Strategic Studies in London reported that the entire

North Korean military budget was $2.1 billion, more than one hundred times less than the Pentagon's annual budget.

11 For more on these points, see William D. Hartung and Michelle Ciarrocca, "Star Wars II: Here We Go Again," *The Nation*, June 19, 2000, and Michelle Ciarrocca and William D. Hartung, *Axis of Influence: Behind the Bush Administration's Missile Defense Revival*, New York World Policy Institute, July 2002.

12 Remarks as Delivered by Secretary of Defense Donald A. Rumsfeld, Washington, DC, November 6, 2001 at the Center for Security Policy "Keeper of the Flame" Award Dinner; also cited in Will S. Hylton, "Dick and Don Go to War," *Esquire*, February 2002.

13 Information on CSP advisory board members and associates with appointments in the Bush administration comes form the Center's 2001 annual report, available at *www.security-policy.org*.

14 Ricard Behar, "Rummy's North Korea Connection—What Did Donald Rumsfeld Know About ABB's Deal to Build Nuclear Reactors There? And Why Won't He Talk About It?," *Fortune*, May 12, 2003.

15 Richard Wolfe, et. al., "Implausible Deniability," *Newsweek International*, April 14, 2003.

4

The Carlyle Group:
Crony Capitalism without Borders

"Carlyle is as deeply wired into the current administration as they can possibly be. George H. W. Bush is getting money from private interests that have business before the government, while his son is President . . . George W. Bush could, some day, benefit from his father's investments . . . that's a jaw-dropper."

—CHUCK LEWIS,
Director, Center for Public Integrity, March 2001

"It screamed conflict-of-interest. We asked publicly that the senior Bush step down. To this day we don't know why he hasn't resigned. It's causing a scandal."

—TOM FITTON, Judicial Watch, November 2001

"Some folks are born, silver spoon in hand, Lord don't they help themselves . . ."

—CREEDENCE CLEARWATER REVIVAL,"Fortunate Son"

 THE CARLYLE GROUP is the most politically connected investment firm in the world. The company has mastered the art of influence peddling on a global scale, hiring executives and

consultants ranging from Republican power broker James Baker and former president George Herbert Walker Bush to foreign leaders like former British prime minister John Major and former Philippine president Fidel Ramos.

Carlyle's CEO, Frank Carlucci, served as secretary of defense and head of the National Security Council under Ronald Reagan and was Rumsfeld's college roommate at Princeton. His special relationship with Rumsfeld puts him in a perfect position to size up U.S. defense policies and programs for purposes of crafting Carlyle's investment strategy. There is circumstantial evidence to suggest that Rumsfeld *has* helped out his old college friend by giving him a heads-up on the likely status of the Crusader artillery system, a major multi-billion dollar project which prior to its cancellation in the spring of 2002 was the most lucrative project at United Defense, a major weapons maker owned by Carlyle.[3]

The President's father, George Herbert Walker Bush, is on retainer to Carlyle, using his reputation and contacts as ex-president to help the firm recruit new investors in the Middle East, Asia, and beyond. He holds meetings with Saudi potentates, makes speeches or plays golf with potential investors in South Korea, and so forth. Press reports indicate that he may receive $100,000 or more a pop for every speech he gives on Carlyle's behalf. "Bush 41" is engaged in Influence Peddling 101, except instead of lobbying the U.S. government to help a specific company or land a specific contract, Carlyle uses its accumulated connections to garner inside information that enables them to "play the market" for defense and security companies. Without its ability to give investors the impression that it has inside dope on the direction of U.S. government policy that no other firm can get, there would be no rationale for the Carlyle Group to exist.

James Baker, whose leadership of the Republican recount effort in Florida in November and December of 2000 paved the way for George W. Bush's selection as president, is a senior counselor with the Carlyle Group. According to Dan Briody's excellent profile of Carlyle, *The Iron Triangle*, it was Baker's addition to the firm in March of 1993 that catapulted it into the top ranks of global investment firms.[4] His political connections, developed during his years as secretary of commerce, secretary of state, and White House chief of staff in the administrations of Ronald Reagan and George H. W. Bush, are unparalleled among his colleagues in the global investment field. Executives like Baker are like gold to a company like Carlyle, which depends on major members of the global political and economic elites to steer business their way. Like Dick Cheney, Baker can parlay the connections he made in Saudi Arabia and other oil-rich Persian Gulf states during the 1991 Gulf War into contracts and investments from a motley array of wealthy sheiks, bankers, and potentates in the region. But instead of shaking them down for contracts to build up their oil facilities, as Cheney and Halliburton have done, Carlyle's key Republican front man tries to persuade his Middle Eastern counterparts to put money into one of the firm's investment funds. In that sense Baker and his colleagues at Carlyle are "confidence men," wooing potential investors with the promise that Carlyle has inside governmental information that can guide them toward rich returns.

Other individuals on Carlyle's team of politically connected advisors are former British prime minister John Major, former Philippines president Fidel Ramos, former South Korean prime minister Park Tae-joon, and former Thai prime minister Anand Panyarachun.[5]

The true story behind Carlyle's ever expanding empire is complex, although not as sinister as some accounts imply. The principals in Carlyle—Frank Carlucci, James Baker, George H. W. Bush—are by and large moderate internationalists who differ in policy and ideology from neo-cons like Frank Gaffney and Paul Wolfowitz. (This may be one case in which corporate influence might actually have a *moderating* effect on the administration of George W. Bush, for the simple reason that global businessmen often take a more sophisticated view of international politics than ideologues of the Frank Gaffney school do. James Baker is no Richard Perle.) H. W. Bush's association with Carlyle drew international attention in the aftermath of September 11 when it was revealed that the construction company owned by Osama bin Laden's family, the Saudi Binladin Group, was an investor in the Carlyle Group. Furthermore, Bush may have been involved in convincing the Saudi conglomerate to place its funds with Carlyle. On September 11, 2001,

Carlyle was in the midst of its annual investors conference at the Ritz-Carlton Hotel in Washington, D.C. At that same meeting, alongside James Baker, Frank Carlucci, and other members in good standing of the world's economic and political elite, was Osama Bin Laden's half-brother, Shafiq Bin Laden. He was there to keep an eye on the Saudi Binladin Group's investment in one of Carlyle's global funds.[6]

On September 27, 2001, the *Wall Street Journal* brought George Herbert Walker Bush's Carlyle connection into the international media spotlight. In an article entitled, "Bin Laden Family is Tied to U.S. Group," Daniel Golden, James Bandler, and Marcus Walker reported that "If the U.S. boosts defense spending in its quest to stop Osama Bin Laden's alleged terrorist activities, there may be one unexpected beneficiary: Mr. Bin Laden's family." They noted that the Saudi Binladin group had invested at least $2 million, and possibly much more, with the Carlyle Group, and it quoted an executive's assertion that the Bin Laden family business was in line to receive a 40 percent rate of return on its investment. It also made clear that George H. W. Bush had met with Bin Laden family members in Saudi Arabia at least twice on Carlyle business, once in 1998 and once in 2000.

The issue at hand in the Binladin Group/Carlyle connection was not whether the President's father was somehow in league with Osama Bin Laden. The Bin Laden family has long since disowned their errant brother. As Charles Freeman, a former U.S. ambassador to Saudi Arabia whose organization, the Middle East Policy Council, receives funding from Bin Laden family members, put it, "They're the establishment that Osama is trying to overthrow."[7] This view was shared by former President Jimmy Carter, who met with ten of Osama's brothers in Saudi Arabia in early 2000 and eventually raised $200,000 from Bin Laden family members for the activities of the Carter Center, his Atlanta-based research and public education organization. But a Bush–Bin Laden business link—even if it was with the "good" Bin Ladens—was more than public opinion would bear. By late October 2001, the Carlyle Group and the Saudi Binladin Group had severed their financial ties. A Carlyle official familiar with the decision told the *Wall Street Journal* that it was driven by "questioning from outside the company about any chance of [the Bin Laden family] profiting because of investments that are going to increase in value because of the war on terrorism."[8] For Carlyle, cutting its ties to the Bin Laden family was a public relations move, not a change of policy or principles. As one Carlyle executive put it when the Bush–Bin Laden link was first revealed, "The situation's changed now. I don't want to spend my life talking to reporters."[9]

Bush the elder has little to say about his Carlyle connection, just as he maintains a carefully controlled silence about what kind of advice he gives his son. But it is precisely this special relationship between Bush 41 and Bush 43 that raises the most troubling questions about Bush senior's position with Carlyle. As Dan Briody notes in *The Iron Triangle*, George H. W. Bush still has access to regular CIA briefings on the state of the world. Although he claims that he doesn't share the details of these briefings with his cronies at Carlyle, the very fact that he has this privileged information means he can steer Carlyle toward certain opportunities, or away from certain companies, based on his special access to classified U.S. government intelligence assessments of key countries, regions, and global trends.[10]

When Dick Cheney was attacked for his revolving door relationship with Halliburton, he hit back at his critics, claiming that his rise to riches as the CEO of an arms and energy conglomerate was "the quintessential American success story." And when former Defense Policy Board chairman Richard Perle was caught not once, not twice, but *three times* with his hands in the cookie jar, using his governmental position to solicit private contracts and investments for his very own Carlyle-style investment group, Trireme, he viciously attacked the journalists who pointed out his conflicts of interest and wrote a lengthy self-justification in the *Wall Street Journal*, arguing that if you want advice from folks who know something about defense, you need to tap people with ties to the defense industry.

While the Carlyle-Bush-Baker-Carlucci-Rumsfeld connections are troubling enough in their own right, they look even worse when you consider how many different ways Carlyle is profiting from the war on terrorism. Speaking in particular about Carlucci and his three main partners at Carlyle, Dan Briody has observed that "It is not an exaggeration to say that September 11 was going to make them very, very rich men."

George W. Bush also had a connection to the company

prior to becoming president. Back in 1990, Carlyle operative Fred Malek brokered Carlyle's purchase of Caterair, a catering outfit that serviced major airlines. One of the people Malek recruited to serve on the Caterair board was George W. Bush. In effect, young Dubya was "Carlyle's man at Caterair." Carlyle's investment in Caterair did not go well, but the precedent of Carlyle reaching out and hiring a member of a sitting president's family had been established.[11]

Currently the company's best-known arms industry investment is United Defense, a joint venture of the FMC and Harsco corporations that specializes in providing armored vehicles and howitzers to the Pentagon. Until recently, United Defense's big "program of the future" was the Crusader artillery system, a complex, heavy-duty long-range howitzer that was being developed as the U.S. Army's next generation artillery piece. To Donald Rumsfeld's credit, he cancelled the project in the spring of 2002 in response to concerns that the Crusader was too bulky to be airlifted to distant combat zones in the U.S. military's existing transport planes. He did so over the objections of his old friend Frank Carlucci and the Carlyle Group, not to mention protests from the top brass of the U.S. Army and key elected officials like Rep. J.C. Watts (R-OK), who was looking forward to having a Crusader assembly facility set up in his congressional district.

The question is, did Donald Rumsfeld give his old friend a heads up so he could milk the Crusader for all it was worth prior to the cancellation? He's not telling. A Pentagon spokesperson claimed that anyone who would even suggest improper collusion "doesn't know Donald Rumsfeld and Frank Carlucci."

Carlyle's handling of its United Defense investment is certainly consistent with the idea of Rumsfeld tipping Carlucci off in advance. Carlyle took United Defense public in December of 2001—less than six months from the time the company's biggest program was cancelled—and raised $237 million. If Rumsfeld had cancelled the Crusader in the spring of 2001 instead of the spring of 2002, United Defense would not have been nearly so attractive an investment for nascent shareholders, and Carlyle probably would have netted much less on its stock offering. As Walter Pincus of the *Washington Post* pointed out, even before the public stock offering Carlyle took out a loan of $600 million to refinance a portion of the original purchase price that it plunked down to buy United Defense, and promptly distributed $387 million of the borrowed funds to executives and shareholders in the form of bonuses and dividends. Pincus also noted that United Defense would be in line for a big fat cancellation fee from the Pentagon in association with the termination of the Crusader. United Defense would also have an inside track on the new artillery system that the Army is planning to build to replace the Crusader.[12]

As this went to press, Carlyle announced that it was planning to "cash out" of United Defense, selling its remaining 20 percent stake in the firm for somewhere in the area of $300 million.[13] The firm will have made back its initial investment many times over.

United Defense is far from being Carlyle's only major holding in the defense and security sector. Other Carlyle investments that are yielding handsome profits from the war on terrorism include USIS, a former federal agency (which has since been privatized) that specializes in vetting personnel for positions in sensitive, security-related jobs. Since the September 11 attacks, USIS's 3,600 employees are doing a booming business in background checks on potential employees for the Pentagon, U.S. intelligence agencies, the Department of Homeland Security, and the commercial airlines.[14]

EG&G, a 4,500 employee company specializing in weapons testing, maintenance, and support services, was a part of the Carlyle family of companies until August of 2002, when the firm sold it to the San Francisco-based engineering conglomerate URS corporation for $675 million.[15] Carlyle's ability to buy a firm like EG&G and then "flip" it a few years later at a profit greatly enhances its ability to profit from U.S. military and security policies by "riding the wave" of government procurement and research priorities, using its roster of influential former government officials to garner the inside information needed to know when to "pull the trigger" on a given investment.

Two other Carlyle-controlled companies, Composite Structures and Vought Aircraft, are well placed to profit from the boom in aerospace spending that has been fostered by the Bush administration's air power-driven regime changes in Afghanistan and Iraq. The two companies are involved in supplying components for everything from the

Army's Apache attack helicopter, to the Air Force's C-117 transport plane, to the B-2 bomber, to both current and next-generation combat jets. With existing aircraft like the Lockheed Martin F-16, the Boeing F-18, and the Lockheed Martin F-117 seeing heavy duty—and undergoing substantial wear and tear—in the air wars in Iraq, suppliers of aircraft components like Composite Structures and Vought are well placed to receive more orders to shore up the Air Force's current inventory. Add to that the Pentagon's three new fighter plane programs—the Lockheed Martin/Boeing F-22 fighter, the Lockheed Martin F-35 Joint Strike Fighter, and the Boeing/Northrop Grumman F/A-18E/F aircraft carrier-based combat aircraft—and the business in supplying parts for new combat planes will increase. Donald Rumsfeld was allegedly going to reconsider the need for three new combat planes during the defense policy review he conducted when the Bush administration first took office, but he lacked the courage to do more than nibble at the edges of these massive programs, which together may cost U.S. taxpayers $350 billion or more over the next two decades. Never mind the fact that neither Iraq, nor the Taliban, nor any of the other countries on the Pentagon's hit list have any real air power to speak of, or that independent studies have shown that our existing combat aircraft fleet, with the occasional upgrade, can guarantee the United States air superiority for the foreseeable future. The Air Force, the contractors, and the members of Congress in states and districts where these planes are built want their pet programs to be funded.

While Composite Structures and Vought supply components for military and civilian aircraft, another Carlyle-owned company, Lier Siegler Services, provides logistical and maintenance services to governments ranging from Saudi Arabia—as part of the Saudi "Peace Hawk" program—to the United States, where it holds Pentagon contracts for work on the F-5 and F-15 combat planes and the Bradley Fighting Vehicle (a product of its fellow Carlyle-owned company, United Defense).

Last but not least, Carlyle's Federal Data Systems Corporation has been described as "the premier provider of information technology services to the U.S. government," with contracts in place with the Internal Revenue Service, the U.S. Air Force, and many other federal agencies.[16]

Not content with its incredible access and influence over the administration of George W. Bush, Carlyle continues to expand aggressively. At the end of the Clinton administration, it picked up two well-connected alumni, outgoing Federal Communications Commission director William Kennard and outgoing Securities and Exchange Commission (SEC) chairman Arthur Levitt, in an effort to "round out" its domestic political portfolio with a few high-profile Democrats. In mid-2002 the company helped launch the China Venture Capital Association, a group that Briody describes as "a nebulous organization charged with warding off corruption in China and strengthening ties with the Chinese government."[17] Later that same year, Carlyle bought Qinetiq, the former research and development arm of the British Ministry of Defense, leading Fiona Draper, a spokesperson for the union that represents the workers at the former government agency, to question whether "given Carlyle's fairly opaque structure, there must be concerns about whether undue influence may be brought to bear on the British government."[18]

At bottom, Carlyle is just an investment firm, with no particular political agenda. However, there is one area where the company's influence could have a negative impact on U.S. security: in our policy toward Saudi Arabia. Not only do many of Carlyle's investors come from the Saudi Kingdom, but for years the company was under contract to run the Saudi "offset" program, a program of targeted investments in Saudi Arabia that recipients of Saudi arms contracts were required to engage in as a condition of sale. For example, when the British government sold Saudi Arabia the Tornado aircraft, or Boeing sold Riyadh a new batch of F-15s, the exporting entity would be required to invest a certain amount of money into the Saudi economy as an "offset" to the billions that the Saudis were spending on foreign aircraft. It was essentially a system of legalized bribery. Carlyle's contract to help the Saudi regime run this program (which has since lapsed) offered its executives all manner of opportunities to influence and approach members of the royal family about investing in one of Carlyle's funds. Its financial links to the Saudi royal family mean that Carlyle does not encourage or cooperate with investigations into Saudi citizens who may have funded or otherwise aided and abetted the September 11 hijackers. Carlyle's ties to wealthy Saudi investors are undoubtedly one of the reasons that the administration of George W. Bush hasn't pressed the Saudi regime more vigorously to supply information on Saudi citizens who may have helped Al Qaeda.[19]

In fact, Carlyle executive and Bush political confidante James Baker is representing key members of the Saudi government against a $1 trillion law suit being brought against them by family members of victims of the September 11 terror attacks. His law firm, Baker Botts, is defending Saudi defense minister Prince Sultan Bin Abdul Aziz against charges that he funneled regular payments to Islamic charities that were fronts for Osama Bin Laden's terror network.[20] The firm is well-positioned to help its Saudi clients. Not only did Baker Botts go to bat for George W. Bush in the Florida recount wars of November and December 2000, but George W. Bush has chosen Bob Jordan, a former partner at Baker Botts, to be his ambassador to Saudi Arabia.[21]

When it comes time to press members of the Saudi elite for cooperation in cutting off the funding sources of Al Qaeda and other terror groups, whose interests will James Baker and Bob Jordan be acting on, their long-time Saudi clients, or America's?

— Chapter 4 Notes —

1   Quoted in Leslie Wayne, "Elder Bush in G.O.P. Cast Toiling for Top Equity Firm," *New York Times*, March 5, 2001.

2   The quote is from Dan Briody, *The Iron Triangle: Inside the Secret World of the Carlyle Group* (Hoboken, New Jersey: John Wiley and Sons, 2003), p. 119.

3   For an overview of the Crusader affair and Rumsfeld and Carlucci's role in it, see William D. Hartung, "Farewell Crusader?–Insiders Will Cash in Regardless," a Foreign Policy in Focus Global Affairs Commentary, May 21, 2002. For an excellent piece on how the Carlyle Group was able to insulate itself from any financial liability associated with the Crusader cancellation, see Walter Pincus, "Crusader a Boon to Carlyle Even If Pentagon Scraps Project," *Washington Post*, May 14, 2002.

4   Dan Briody, *The Iron Triangle*, op. cit., pp. 70–74 and 80–89; for the best quick overview of Carlyle's operations, see Tim Shorrock, "Crony Capitalism Goes Global," *The Nation*, April 1, 2002.

5   Dan Briody, *The Iron Triangle*, op. cit., pages 89 and 113.

6   Briody, *The Iron Triangle*, pp. 139–140.

7   Daniel Golden, James Bandler, and Marcus Walker, "Bin Laden Family Is Tied to U.S. Group," *Wall Street Journal*, September 27, 2001.

8   "Bin Laden Family Ends Carlyle Group Relationship," *Wall Street Journal*, October 29, 2001.

9   Golden, et. al., "Bin Laden Family is Tied to U.S. Group," op. cit.

10 Dan Briody, *The Iron Triangle*, op. cit., p. 120.

11 This is the same Fred Malek who was forced to step down as chairman of the Republican National Committee when it was revealed that he had presided over a purge of Jewish staffers at the Bureau of Labor Statistics in the early 1970s at the instruction of Richard Nixon. See Dan Briody, op. cit., pp. 13–21.

12 See Walter Pincus, "Crusader a Boon to Carlyle," op. cit.; and William D. Hartung, " Farewell Crusader?—Insiders Will Cash in Regardless," op. cit.

13 Jo Johnson, "Carlyle to Sell Remaining Stake in United Defence," *Financial Times* (London), September 22, 2003.

14 Unless otherwise noted, the thumbnail sketches of Carlyle-owned companies in this section are drawn from Dan Briody's excellent synopsis in *The Iron Triangle*, op. cit., pages 161–164.

15 URS Corporation, "URS Completes Acquisition of EG&G Technical Services," August 22, 2002.

16 Dan Briody, *The Iron Triangle*, op. cit., p. 163.

17 Dan Briody, op. cit., p. 156.

18 Dan Briody, op. cit., p. 157.

19 On the Saudi connection, see Jonathan Wells, Jack Meyers, and Maggie Mulvihill, "U.S. Ties to Saudi Elite May Be Hurting War on Terrorism," *Boston Herald*, December 10, 2001, and "Bush Advisors Cashed in On Saudi Gravy Train," by the same authors, *Boston Herald*, December 11, 2001 (the two-part series is posted on the progressive web site www.commondreams.org, where it was posted on December 21, 2001).

20 Michael Isikoff and Mark Hosenball, "A Legal Counterattack," *Newsweek* web exclusive, April 16, 2003.

21 Baker Botts L.L.P. Media Center, "President Bush to Nominate Bob Jordan to Be Ambassador of the United States to Saudi Arabia," July 17, 2001; and " Jordan Confirmed as Ambassador to Saudi Arabia," October 5, 2001.

5

The Defense Policy Board: Richard Perle and His Merry Band of Profiteers

 **FEW AMERICANS HAD** heard of the Defense Policy Board (DPB) until Richard Perle was forced to step down as its chairman in the spring of 2003. He was charged with abusing his position as a top advisor to Secretary of Defense Donald Rumsfeld for personal gain. Although he chose the self-imposed "punishment" of stepping down from the chairmanship of the Defense Policy Board, he refused to admit to any wrongdoing, and did not give up his seat as a regular member of the board.

Amidst the alphabet soup of advisory boards that have been created over the years to provide independent perspectives to the secretary of defense, the secretary of state, and the president—from the Defense Science Board (DSB), to the President's Foreign Intelligence Advisory

Board (PFIAB), to the State Department's Defense Trade Advisory Group (DTAG)—the DPB is first among equals in the eyes of the Bush administration.

Under the leadership of Donald Rumsfeld and Richard Perle, the DSB has been transformed from a nonpartisan advisory body designed to give the secretary of defense a broader range of views on pressing security issues into a megaphone for the rigid policy preferences of the secretary of defense. In the run-up to the March 2003 U.S. intervention in Iraq, Perle, former CIA Director R. James Woolsey, former Reagan administration Arms Control and Disarmament Agency head Kenneth Adelman, former House Speaker Newt Gingrich, and the other appointees to the thirty-member DSB were all over the press and television, stumping for Donald Rumsfeld and Paul Wolfowitz's war.

Perle is one of the most viciously partisan operatives in Washington, a true believer in neo-conservative causes who has worked alongside Rumsfeld for more than two decades. He served on the advisory board of Rumsfeld's favorite right-wing think tank, Frank Gaffney's right-wing Center for Security Policy (CSP).

In addition to their CSP connection, both Perle and Rumsfeld signed the June 1997 founding "statement of principles" of the Project for the New American Century (PNAC). This statement, which calls for a return to "a Reaganite policy of military strength and moral clarity," has become the de facto gospel for the resurgent neo-conservative movement.[1] Long before the September 11 attacks were used as a rationale for shifting toward a doctrine of "preventive war," Perle, Rumsfeld and their PNAC pals were touting regime change and peace through strength as essential elements of a new U.S. security policy.

On March 17, 2003, veteran investigative reporter Seymour Hersh reported in the *The New Yorker* that Perle used his position as chairman of the DPB to solicit $100 million for his security-oriented investment firm, Trireme, which was his own personal version of the Carlyle Group. But unlike the principals at Carlyle, who at least had the decency to wait until they left government service to cash in on their connections, Perle was attempting to capitalize while still serving as an official advisor to Secretary of Defense Donald Rumsfeld.

Hersh described how Perle had used Adnan Khashoggi, the notorious Saudi arms middleman who was involved in the 1980s Iran/Contra scandal, to arrange a meeting with Harb Saleh al-Zuhair, "a Saudi industrialist whose family fortune includes extensive holdings in construction, electronics, and engineering companies throughout the Middle East."[2] The Saudi businessman *thought* he was being invited to lunch with the DPB chairman in Marseilles, in the south of France—where the inveterate France-basher maintains a home—to get Perle's reaction to a peace plan designed to head off U.S. intervention in Iraq by arranging for Saddam Hussein's exile. In fact Perle was more interested in seeing whether Al-Zuhair and nine Saudi colleagues might invest $10 million each into Trireme. Al-Zuhair and Khashoggi assert that the solicitation of funds for Trireme was the main point of the meeting, a claim that Perle denied to Hersh. But Perle's denial is undercut by the fact that Adnan Khashoggi was sent a two-page solicitation letter prior to the lunch meeting which mentions that "Three of Trireme's Management Group members currently advise the U.S. Secretary of Defense by serving on the U.S. Defense Policy Board, and one of Trireme's principals, Richard Perle, is chairman of that Board." That certainly sounds like the prelude to a pitch.

The Saudi ambassador in Washington, Prince Bandar Bin Sultan—a world-class wheeler-dealer in his own right—who heard about the meeting through his own sources in Saudi Arabia, asserted that the discussion of the peace plan was just a "cover story" to provide "deniability" for Perle, stating, "I believe the Iraqi events are irrelevant. A business meeting took place."[3] If the alleged sales pitch had come to fruition, it would have been a great coup for Perle's fledgling firm. An influx of $100 million in Saudi funds into Trireme would have more than doubled the firm's capital, which as of the spring of 2003 was only $45 million.

Trireme was only incorporated in November 2001, *after* Perle was appointed chairman of the DPB by Rumsfeld and *after* the September 11 terror attacks set the stage for massive increases in military and security spending.

Perle also managed to get one of his business associates, Gerald Hillman, who also happens to run Trireme's New York office, appointed to the Defense Policy Board. Several members of the board told Hersh that they were not aware of Perle's Trireme connection, nor did they know that Hillman was involved with the firm. One member of the

DPB told Hersh that this was so over the line as to be virtually unbelievable: "Oh, get out of here. He's the chairman! If you had a story about me setting up a company for homeland security, and I've put people on the [Defense Policy] board I'm doing business with . . . I think it would stink to high heaven."[4]

Perle felt otherwise. When Wolf Blitzer asked Perle about Hersh's allegations on his Sunday newsmaker interview show on CNN, Perle went on the attack, calling Hersh "the closest thing we have in American journalism to a terrorist."

The next scandal to emerge was revealed by Stephen Labaton for the *New York Times*. In a deal that may even surpass his Adnan Khashoggi connection for sheer chutzpah, Perle offered his services to the corrupt, bankrupt telecommunications firm, Global Crossing, with a promise to get them U.S. government approval for the sale of one of their business units to a Chinese-owned company. Sales of high-tech assets to potential adversaries like China must be cleared by the Committee on Foreign Investment in the United States (C.F.I.U.S.), which includes representatives from the Pentagon, the FBI, and other federal agencies. In an affidavit that appears to have been used in soliciting Global Crossing's business, Perle stated that, "As the chairman of the Defense Policy Board, I have a unique perspective on and intimate knowledge of the national defense and security issues that will be raised by the C.F.I.U.S. review process that is not and could not be available to the other C.F.I.U.S. professionals."[5] Perle had originally denied trading on his DPB post in his pitch to Global Crossing, then backtracked once he realized that Labaton had a copy of his signed affidavit. Perle's fallback was to say that the reference to the board was a "clerical error," and that he had in fact asked his lawyers to remove it, and later neglected to check this before signing the document.

Perle had stood to gain a $600,000 incentive payment on top of his $125,000 base fee if the sale of the Global Crossing unit to the Chinese-owned company was approved by the C.F.I.U.S.

Further digging by Labaton and others revealed that during the latter part of 2001, Perle was employed by another company, the Loral Corporation. Loral had been charged with the improper transfer of satellite information to Beijing, which had the potential to improve the accuracy and range of China's nuclear-armed ballistic missiles (twenty of which are currently able to reach targets in the United States). Secretary of State Colin Powell admitted that Perle had made several calls on Loral's behalf to Lincoln Bloomfield, the official in charge of deciding whether the company had cleaned up its act vis-à-vis technology transfers to China. Perle allowed that he had weighed in with Bloomfield "relat[ing] to the licensing" of future Loral satellite technology sales to China, but he claimed that he was "not compensated by the company in connection with that activity."[6] However, he *was* a paid consultant to the firm, and any efforts he may have made on their behalf on the satellite export issue no doubt reminded them of his future value to the company.

Perle is also on the board of directors of FNSS, a Turkish

armored vehicle maker that produces U.S.-designed combat systems under license from U.S. arms maker United Defense; and the Autonomy Corporation, a British firm that holds a major U.S. government contract for work on homeland defense.

Perle's business ties are a work in progress, since he literally never seems to stop promoting himself for a fee. A former member of the Defense Policy Board who sat behind him on a New York to Washington flight during the early part of his tenure as chairman reports that Perle spent the whole flight pitching a Japanese businessman on either investing with Trireme or hiring Perle as a consultant. Perle didn't realize that his DPB colleague was sitting behind him until the flight landed, at which point he became quite animated and defensive, claiming that the discussion was not what it sounded like. Ari Berman revealed in an editorial that ran in *The Nation* in the summer of 2003 that Perle has made it a practice to routinely ask foreign broadcasting outlets for a fee in exchange for interviews soliciting his views as the chairman of the Defense Policy Board. The amounts involved ranged from $100 to $900 per interview. Berman suggests that Perle's solicitation of fees appears to violate U.S. government regulations for Special Government Employees (SGE's) against using their public position for private gain. As former DPB board member Barry Blechman put it, "It's naïve to say [TV stations] weren't more interested in Perle because he was chairman. If [TV] says we want the chairman and from that basis he wanted a fee, it would be prohibited." When asked to comment on all of this, Perle stated, "The suggestion that being paid for work I do is somehow an abuse of my role as a member of a government advisory board is the sort of slander I expect from *The Nation*, which, since the collapse of regard for the vision of its founders, and the paucity of ideas to replace it, has been reduced to impugning the character of those whose ideas have prevailed over yours."[7]

Just as Perle was stepping down as the chairman of DPB, the Washington-based Center for Public Integrity released a report indicating that he was not alone among his colleagues on the board in taking an active role as an arms industry consultant, executive, and investment advisor while serving as a close advisor to Donald Rumsfeld. The Center found that nine of the board's thirty members had relationships with weapons contractors that together had received over $76 billion in contracts from the Pentagon in the most recent year for which figures are available. Perle's partners in influence-peddling include his neo-con fellow traveler R. James Woolsey, who runs the Global Strategic Security practice for Booz Allen Hamilton, a beltway bandit which bagged $680 million in Pentagon contracts in Fiscal Year 2002; Jack Sheehan, a retired general who works for Bechtel, which is currently cashing in on the rebuilding of Iraq; David Jeremiah, a retired admiral with ties to the Mitre Corporation, a major Pentagon R&D contractor, which is run by fellow DPB board member James Schlesinger, who served as defense secretary prior to Donald Rumsfeld's first go-round at the job back in the mid-1970s.[8]

In a defensive editorial that ran in the *Wall Street Journal*, entitled "Center for Public Ignorance," the journal ridiculed the Center's findings, arguing that since the DPB members serve without pay there is nothing inherently wrong with them making a living as consultants, executives, or investment advisors in the fields of defense and homeland security.[9]

In a self-serving apologia that ran on the same page of the *Journal*, Perle noted that "the people best able to help" government policymakers in an advisory capacity "are professionally involved with the businesses for which the official is responsible: health professionals or pharmaceutical executives advising the Department of Health and Human Services, for example, or energy executives advising the Department of Energy, or defense executives advising the Department of Defense."[10]

He suggested that rules about disclosure of financial interests by advisory panel members and "recusal" from decisions involving specific companies a board member may be involved in provide adequate safeguards against someone like himself using his public position for private gain. But as Seymour Hersh's expose demonstrated, a number of Perle's colleagues on the board were not aware of his financial stake in Trireme.

Perle's final point was that "an advisor following these rules [of disclosure and recusal from matters affecting companies he or she does business with] should be free to give his best candid advice." However this "candid advice" led Perle and his DPB colleague Kenneth Adelman to suggest that the U.S. intervention in Iraq would be a "cakewalk" (Adelman's phrase, echoed by Perle in different language).

It was Perle and his DPB partner in crime R. James Woolsey who alleged links between Al Qaeda and Saddam Hussein. It was Perle and his colleagues at the DPB who suggested that Saddam Hussein's forces possessed nuclear, chemical, and biological weapons that posed an imminent threat to the United States. And it was Perle and Undersecretary of Defense for Policy Douglas Feith who have pressed most vigorously for a U.S.-backed puppet government led by the Iraqi exile Ahmed Chalabi, a high-living, alleged embezzler who had not stepped inside the country for forty-five years before the Pentagon dropped him in behind U.S. lines during the early stages of "Operation Iraqi Freedom."

Perle's advice on Iraq has been wrong on all counts. Professional intelligence analysts in the United States, the United Kingdom, and around the world have persuasively argued that there were no operational links between Saddam Hussein and Al Qaeda prior to the spring 2003 U.S.-led invasion of Iraq. U.S. forces failed to find workable nuclear, chemical, or biological weapons in Iraq after taking control of the country. U.S. forces dispatched Saddam Hussein's regime relatively quickly, but it was far from the "cakewalk" that Perle and company—echoed by high administration officials and allies like Deputy Defense Secretary Paul Wolfowitz and Vice President Dick Cheney—claimed it would be. The Iraqi people have not arisen as one to welcome U.S. forces as liberators, and more U.S. troops have died in the occupation phase of the war than were killed in the period leading up to the collapse of the regime of Saddam Hussein. The costs of the war—in lives and dollars—are already several orders of magnitude higher than the neo-con brigades claimed they would be. And United States forces will be bogged down in Iraq for many more months to come.

Despite this record of bad advice—which has undermined the security of our nation and the safety of our troops—Donald Rumsfeld sang Perle's praises when he stepped down as chair of the DPB, calling him a man of "deep integrity and honor," with a "deep understanding of our national security process." Not only did Rumsfeld fail to acknowledge that his long-time fellow partisan had done anything wrong, but his high praise for Perle sounds like it could have been lifted straight from a letter of recommendation. I wouldn't be surprised if Rumsfeld's words, or a summary thereof, appear in one of Perle's future pitch letters for Trireme.

— Chapter 5 Notes —

1 Statement of Principles, Project for the New American Century,
   June 3, 1997, available on the web at
   www.newamericancentury.org/statementofprinciples.htm
2   Seymour M. Hersh, "Lunch With the Chairman," *The New
   Yorker*, March 17, 2003.
3 Seymour Hersh, "Lunch With the Chairman," op. cit.
4 Seymour Hersh, "Lunch With the Chairman," op. cit. The brack-
   eted words were not in the original article, but have been added
   for clarity—to make clear that "the board" being referred to is
   the Defense Policy Board, not the board of directors of Trireme.
5 Stephen Labaton and Thom Shanker, "After Disclosures, Pentagon
   Adviser Quits a Post," *New York Times*, March 28, 2003.
6 Stephen Labaton, "Perle Advised Firm Accused of Giving China
   Technology," *Houston Chronicle*, March 29, 2003.
7 The quotes in this section are from Ari Berman, "Payments for
   Perle," *The Nation*, August 18–25, 2003.
8 For the best summary of the Center for Public Integrity report
   and additional arms industry links of DPB members, see Tim
   Shorrock, "Richard Perle's Corporate Adventures," *The Nation*
   (web only), April 3, 2003.
9 "Center for Public Ignorance," *Wall Street Journal*, March 31, 2003.
10 Richard Perle, "For the Record," *Wall Street Journal*, March 31,
   2003.

Policy Profiteers: The Role of Right-Wing Think Tanks in Shaping Bush's Foreign Policy

"I support a zero option for all nuclear weapons . . . my dream is to see the day when all nuclear weapons are banished from the face of the earth."

— PRESIDENT RONALD REAGAN, January 16, 1984

"The fact is, I see no compelling reason why we should not unilaterally get rid of our nuclear weapons. To maintain them is costly and adds nothing to our security."

— PAUL NITZE, former Reagan arms control negotiator, *New York Times*, 10/29/99

"I view our nuclear arsenal as a deterrent. . . . And the president must have all options available to make that deterrent have meaning."

— PRESIDENT GEORGE W. BUSH, responding to a question about plans to develop "low-yield" nuclear weapons, 3/13/02

 A FUNNY THING happened on the way to the Reagan revolution. Before Reagan took charge in Washington in January

1981, the right-wing Heritage Foundation published a voluminous blueprint for conservative rule known as the *Mandate for Change*. The conservative movement was fervently hoping that Reagan would treat this study, which included all of their pet projects and programs, as the bible of his new administration.

It ended up, however, that on key issues, most notably the issue of nuclear weapons and nuclear strategy, Ronald Reagan had a mind of his own. And Reagan's ideas on the nuclear issue were about as far as you could get from the chest-thumping, unreconstructed arms-racing mentality of the denizens of the Heritage Foundation and its brethren among Washington's growing crop of hard-line conservative organizations. Leon V. Sigal has summed up Reagan's "nuclear radicalism" as follows:

> Reagan was a man of strong beliefs, and one of them was that the world should get rid of all nuclear weapons, starting with the United States and the Soviet Union. He intuitively grasped two essential points understood by all presidents since Truman, that the nuclear balance is inherently precarious and that nuclear deterrence is potentially suicidal. He put his insight into words: 'A nuclear war can never be won and must never be fought.' That insight opened the way for a radical reduction in nuclear arms.[1]

It was Reagan's advocacy of deep nuclear reductions, as we noted earlier, that led neo-conservative hard-liners like

Frank Gaffney to jump ship and take cover in the world of right-wing think tanks to advocate views that were at root the polar opposite of what Reagan was calling for. But as I also noted, the Gaffney crowd will never admit that they are undercutting the Reagan legacy. They prefer to pretend that Reagan the nuclear abolitionist never existed.

The Reagan experience suggests that while right-wing think tanks can say whatever they want, that is no guarantee that their ideas will prevail once "one of their own" becomes president. But so far at least, George W. Bush looks like a better bet than Ronald Reagan to give the right-wing think tanks and their corporate funders what they want. In fact, Dubya has been single-minded in the pursuit of the most conservative elements of his program, from tax cuts for the rich, to privatization of government services, to deployment of a multi-billion dollar missile defense scheme, to his first-strike, "war without end" military posture.

Where do the Bush administration's ideas come from? In part, Bush has had a strong neo-Reaganite conservative streak in him from the outset. Bush's strongly felt conservative views are bound to have an impact on the direction of his administration, especially at moments when his advisors may disagree.

Beyond the mind of George W. Bush—a limited resource, no matter how you slice it—there is another key set of sources for his administration's elaborately detailed, right-wing policy agenda. Conservative think tanks and advocacy groups like the American Enterprise Institute (AEI), the Center for Security Policy (CSP), the Jewish

Institute for National Security Affairs (JINSA), the National Institute for Public Policy, and the Project for the New American Century have developed both the key outlines and many of the specific details of the Bush administration's policies on nuclear weapons, missile defense, and fighting terrorism.

Far from representing a continuation of Reagan's vision, as they claim to do, these groups represent the views of unreconstructed neo-conservative hard-liners like Frank Gaffney, Richard Perle, and John Bolton, men whose most hawkish instincts were held in check by both Ronald Reagan and George Herbert Walker Bush. By appointing policy-makers from these groups to top positions in his administration, and taking their advice in preference to the advice offered by career professionals in the military, intelligence, and foreign service communities, George W. Bush is leading a counter-revolution in Republican thinking on security issues. His neo-con advisors have all of the zeal of revolutionaries, but their policy preferences are straight out of the sixteenth century—they're like feudal lords armed with nuclear weapons.

If you look beyond the rhetoric to the substance of his policies, George W. Bush's administration is radically out of step with the best traditions of every other Republican administration of the post–World War II era, from Dwight Eisenhower and Richard Nixon on through to Ronald Reagan and "Poppy" Bush.

The most dangerous Bush administration break with the policies of his Republican predecessors has been in the realm of nuclear weapons policy. Under the sway of neo-conservatives like Frank Gaffney and Dr. Keith Payne of the National Institute for Public Policy (NIPP), George W. Bush has junked the Anti-Ballistic Missile Treaty of 1972, the treaty that was negotiated and signed by the administration of that old red, Richard Nixon. More ominously, Team Bush has set the stage for a new, multi-sided nuclear arms race by advocating the development of a new generation of nuclear weapons and expanding the range of scenarios in which the United States might use, or threaten to use, nuclear weapons.[2]

The Bush nuclear doctrine expands the group of nations that are explicitly acknowledged to be on the list of potential U.S. nuclear targets, going well beyond major nuclear-armed states like Russia and China to include nuclear "wannabes" and non-nuclear nations like Iran, Iraq, Syria, and North Korea. The Bush policy also broadens the range of circumstances under which U.S. nuclear weapons may be used. Bush policy-makers advocate using or threatening to use nuclear weapons in the following scenarios: 1) an attack on a nation that has used chemical or biological weapons against U.S. troops or U.S. citizens; 2) a response to an attack on Israel by Iraq or another Arab state; 3) a military conflict over the status of Taiwan; 4) a North Korean attack on South Korea; or, 5) a response to "surprising military developments."[3]

Although Pentagon war-planners have never ruled out scenarios of this sort, no administration since the height of the 1950s anti-Communist hysteria has been so willing to publicly entertain so many different potential uses of nuclear weapons. As William Arkin has aptly put it, the Bush doctrine "reverses an almost two-decades-long trend of relegating nuclear weapons to the category of weapons of last resort."[4]

Just as Bush's decision to trash the ABM Treaty and embark on the deployment of a multi-billion dollar missile defense program tracks closely with the recommendations of Frank Gaffney's Center for Security Policy, the Bush administration's first strike nuclear doctrine owes a great debt to the work of Dr. Keith Payne's National Institute for Public Policy (NIPP).

In January 2001, the same month that Bush took office, the NIPP issued a report entitled "Rationale and Requirements for U.S. Nuclear Forces and Arms Control."[5] The study director was Dr. Keith Payne, whose prior claim to fame was co-authoring, with nuclear doomsday theorist extraordinaire Colin Gray, a 1980 essay on U.S. nuclear strategy that appeared in *Foreign Policy* magazine under the bracing title "Victory Is Possible." Back then, Payne and Gray were arguing that in order to have a "credible" deterrent, the United States must develop concrete plans to fight and win a nuclear war. Otherwise, the argument went, other nations wouldn't believe our threats of nuclear retaliation, and they would feel free to attack U.S. personnel, allies, or territory without fear of a devastating counterattack. Among the essay's more controversial points was its claim that since U.S. casualties in a nuclear exchange could be limited to "only" 20 million people, the notion that a nuclear war is "unwinnable" should be re-thought.[6]

Once one of our most hard-line presidents of the modern era, Ronald Reagan, declared that a nuclear war could never be won and must never be fought, I assumed that folks like Keith Payne and Colin Gray had been permanently marginalized. I was dead wrong. Like so many of his neo-con cohorts, Payne was merely biding his time, honing his positions at a right-wing think tank and hoping to bring about a day in which his aggressive nuclear policy positions would be relevant again in Washington, carried forward by an aggressive, neo-con president. While the NIPP report is couched in the sober language of a policy tract rather than the livelier rhetoric reserved for a policy essay, its core arguments are remarkably similar to the themes outlined in Payne and Gray's 1980 essay on the art of the "winnable" nuclear conflict. The report, which has been by and large incorporated into the Bush administration's official revision of United States nuclear doctrine, stresses the notion of maximum "flexibility" for U.S. nuclear policy-makers. By flexibility, the NIPP report means the flexibility to build up or cut back the U.S. nuclear arsenal as needed, without regard to "rigid" nuclear arms control treaties like the ABM accord or the Strategic Arms Reduction Treaties (START); the flexibility to test and develop new types of nuclear weapons like the low-yield, bunker-busting, "mini-nukes" that have been advocated by the Bush administration as a tool for going after alleged underground nuclear, chemical, and biological weapons facilities; and the "flexibility" that comes from engaging in an across-the-board modernization and upgrading of America's multi-billion dollar nuclear weapons complex.

The neo-cons are no longer on the outside shouting in, as they were in the Clinton/Gore and George H. W. Bush administrations. They are now on the inside making policy. Keith Payne, along with several key members of the panel that issued NIPP's January 2001 report, have been selected for key policy-making and advisory positions in the Bush administration. Keith Payne has served on the Pentagon's "Deterrence Concepts Advisory Panel," which deals with how best to implement the administration's aggressive new nuclear theology. He also served a brief stint as a full-time Pentagon employee, working on nuclear policy issues "inside the building" before heading back out the revolving door to NIPP. [7]

The NIPP report, and the Bush nuclear directive that draws upon it, is nothing less than a bailout plan for the nuclear weapons industry. New types of nuclear weapons, a multi-billion dollar rebuilding plan for the nuclear weapons complex, and a renewed role for nuclear threats in our national security posture all add up to a bonanza for contractors like Bechtel and Lockheed Martin that are intimately involved with the development, testing, and production of nuclear weapons and nuclear delivery vehicles.[8]

Bechtel will profit in its role as the lead partner in Bechtel Nevada, a consortium consisting of Bechtel, Johnson Controls, and Lockheed Martin that has the contract for operating the National Nuclear Security Administration's Nevada Test Site. If the neo-cons get their way and the Bush administration breaks the moratorium on underground nuclear testing, Bechtel and its corporate partners will be swimming in dough. And even if the voluntary ban on underground tests holds firm, there will be billions flowing to the Nevada Test Site to refine U.S. capabilities for so-called "sub-critical" testing. These are nuclear weapons tests that are carried out at low enough levels that they are viewed by some (mostly in the weapons industry) as acceptable even during a global moratorium on testing.[9]

While Bechtel will do just fine under the Bush/NIPP nuclear doctrine, Lockheed Martin will do even better. In addition to its role in running the Nevada Test Site, Lockheed Martin pulls down close to $2 billion per year to run the New Mexico-based Sandia Laboratories, a nuclear weapons design and engineering facility. Just in case the company isn't wired enough already in the nuclear weapons sphere, a former Lockheed Martin executive, Everet Beckner, has been brought on by the Bush administration to serve as the administrator for defense programs at the Department of Energy's National Nuclear Security Administration (NNSA). So, if Lockheed Martin runs into any trouble with its nuclear weapons contracts with NNSA, it has the comfort of knowing that one of its former employees is running the government's nuclear weapons complex.[10]

On the weapons delivery side of the equation, the company's Sunnyvale, California facility is still producing the Trident submarine-launched ballistic missile (SLBM), a multi-warhead, long-range nuclear-armed missile that is considered to be the most secure "leg" of the U.S. nuclear deterrent. The other "legs" of what has come to be known as the U.S. nuclear "triad"—land-based missiles and aircraft-based bombs and cruise missiles—are thought to be more vulnerable to a preemptive strike. Why any leader would be suicidal enough to launch a nuclear attack on the United States, with its thousands of nuclear weapons and vast margin of nuclear overkill, has never been adequately explained by the members of the nuclear priesthood.

The NIPP keeps a lower public profile than its ideological counterpart, the Center for Security Policy. The folks at NIPP prefer to posture their group as an "objective" think tank, rather than adopting the more activist, advocacy tactics favored by Frank Gaffney's CSP. But despite their tactical differences, NIPP and CSP are branches of the same neo-con tree. Like CSP, NIPP depends on hard-right foundations and individual donors for the bulk of its support. Like CSP, NIPP has close links to the weapons companies and laboratories that stand to gain from the policies it advocates. Members in good standing of the nuclear weapons complex who have served on both the CSP and NIPP advisory or governing boards include Kathleen C. Bailey, who spent six years as an analyst at the Lawrence Livermore Laboratory, a nuclear weapons research lab run for the Department of Energy by the University of California; Henry Cooper, a former top missile defense official in the Bush the elder administration, who now runs the missile defense advocacy group High Frontier; Charles Kupperman, the vice president for National Missile Defense programs at Lockheed Martin; and Robert Barker, a thirty-year veteran of the Lawerence Livermore nuclear weapons labs.[11]

The only real difference between Gaffney and CSP and Payne and NIPP comes in how shameless they are in touting their corporate connections. In its 1998 annual report, Gaffney's group listed virtually every weapons-maker that had supported it from its founding, from Lockheed, Martin Marietta, Northrop, Grumman, and Boeing, to the later "merged" incarnations of same—Lockheed Martin, Northrop Grumman, and so forth. Gaffney also produced charts indicating that about one quarter of his group's annual income comes from corporations. Under fire for these connections, Gaffney has suggested that only about half of his corporate revenues come from weapons contractors, as if this somehow gives him a clean bill of ethical health.

By contrast, NIPP is far less forthcoming about its funding sources, merely indicating that "the National Institute research and educational program is supported by government, corporate, and private foundation grants."[12] Given the benefits that major weapons-makers are reaping from the policies that NIPP promotes—and the presence of a Lockheed Martin executive on the organization's board—it would be surprising if NIPP was not on the receiving end of significant donations from arms industry companies and arms industry executives. But unlike their colleague Frank Gaffney, they're too chicken to let on, one way or the other.

Having seen Gaffney and Payne operate, I have no doubt that they would be flaunting the same right-wing nonsense with or without the added incentive of wanting to please their corporate donors. The real problem with the corporate money that goes to groups like CSP and NIPP is that it amplifies the voices of guys like Frank Gaffney and Keith Payne in the national policy debate. By providing them with a substantial portion of the funds they need to run their organizations, companies like Lockheed Martin and Boeing help give ideological hacks like Frank Gaffney or Keith Payne an aura of respectability that their dangerously hare-brained positions on the issues wouldn't otherwise warrant. It also gives weapons-makers like Lockheed Martin and Boeing the fig leaf to influence the national political debate indirectly, by giving the Gaffney and Payne gangs the money they need to promote their pro-military, anti-arms control, rabidly right-wing views. If those same views were stated directly by an executive at Lockheed Martin or Boeing, they would be written off as self-serving pap. But if they can be packaged as the views of a representative of an allegedly unbiased "think tank" like CSP or NIPP, the same corporate propaganda can make a far greater incision into the public and media debates.

At a minimum, groups like CSP and NIPP should be required to make regular reports on how much they are getting from corporations and individuals with a vested interest in the policies they are promoting. And the mainstream press should stop treating them like objective analysts, and report instead that they are officers of think tanks that are funded in part by the arms industry.

I'd like to see Gaffney and his ilk forced to introduce themselves as if they were standing in front of their first Alcoholics Anonymous meeting: "Hi, I'm Frank Gaffney, and I'm funded by Lockheed Martin." This would obviously be a much less neutral-sounding introduction than saying "I'm from the Center for Security Policy" or "I'm from the National Institute for Public Policy." But it would be a hell of a lot more honest.

To take the Alcoholics Anonymous analogy one step further, groups like CSP and NIPP should kick their habit of accepting contributions from weapons companies that stand to gain from the policies their organizations are pushing. Then they might deserve to be treated as unbiased, or at least "unbought," analysts of key security issues. (Somehow, I don't think Frank and Keith are hurrying to take me up on my suggestions, but it's the thought that counts, right?)

Nuclear policy isn't the only area of Bush policy that shows the marks of neo-cons run amok. The Bush administration's policy of "regime change" in Iraq and beyond was prefigured in a series of reports, policy analyses, forums, op-ed pieces, and media interviews by the principals of three other think tanks that are also well represented on Team Bush: the American Enterprise Institute (AEI), the Jewish Institute for National Security Affairs (JINSA), and the Project for the New American Century.

The American Enterprise Institute (AEI) is where Dick and Lynne Cheney and ultra-right State Department arms control official John Bolton hung their hats before the inauguration of the George W. Bush regime in January of 2001. Richard Perle has long-standing ties to the group as well.

One of AEI's many claims to fame—or infamy, depending upon your perspective—has been its long-standing support for the Iraqi National Congress (INC). The INC is an

Iraqi exile group headed by Ahmed Chalabi. The best that can be said about Chalabi is that he is a sunshine patriot, an accused embezzler, and a veteran of the right-wing cocktail party circuit whose exaggerated tales of Iraqi weapons of mass destruction provided much of the ammunition that Rumsfeld, Cheney, and Wolfowitz used to stoke the fires for the 2003 U.S. military intervention in Iraq.

From 1998 on, when there was U.S. government money openly available to support the Iraqi opposition to Saddam Hussein due to the AEI-backed Iraqi Liberation Act, Chalabi's INC grabbed the bulk of the funding. But not everyone was as enamored of Chalabi's leadership abilities as his patrons at AEI and the Pentagon—the State Department actually cut off the organization's American funding prior to "Gulf War II" on the grounds that the funds were not being adequately accounted for. Maybe Chalabi was channeling the money into activities focusing on Iraq, or maybe he was spending it on wining and dining folks in Washington, London, and other far -flung capitals. No one could really tell for sure, so the State Department cut off the INC's funding.

The State Department's rebuke of the INC didn't hurt his standing with the AEI crowd. If anything, it may have helped it. Under the Rumsfeld bureaucratic doctrine—which bears an eerie resemblance to the old Chinese dictum "the enemy of my enemy is my friend"—the fact that Colin Powell and the folks at State had "issues" with Mr. Chalabi probably only increased the INC's standing among the neo-cons. While Rumsfeld and his flunky Douglas Feith, the undersecretary of defense for policy, were busy vetoing most of Powell's suggestions for veteran diplomats to play a part in the Pentagon-run Iraqi provisional authority that took power in Iraq after Saddam Hussein's regime collapsed, they found time to have Chalabi and a bunch of his armed retainers dropped into Iraq, courtesy of the Pentagon. And it came as no surprise to those who know how Rumsfeld's mind works that "his" man in Baghdad, Mr. Chalabi, was the first Iraqi to sit as chair of the rotating "governing council" for Iraq, a body consisting mostly of Iraqi exiles handpicked by Wolfowitz, Feith, and Rumsfeld in the hopes that they will form the core of a new Iraqi government.

Meanwhile, back at AEI, Newt Gingrich, a card-carrying member of Rumsfeld's Defense Policy Board, gave a speech in which he lambasted the State Department for its alleged misdeeds in the run-up to the war with Iraq. In Gingrich's Alice-in-Wonderland view of the world, it was Colin Powell's forlorn efforts to build a coalition through diplomacy that were the cause of whatever problems the United States may have encountered in Iraq, not the Pentagon and the White House's ham-handed, "Ugly-American"-style approach to coalition building. Al Hunt of the *Wall Street Journal* wondered out loud whether Rumsfeld had put his trusted advisor and confidant Gingrich up to slamming Powell. Hunt went on to suggest that "If Newt Gingrich stays on [the Defense Policy Board], it will tell us a lot about Donald Rumsfeld."[13] Gingrich is still on the DPB, and Rumsfeld is still trying to undermine his own administration's top diplomat, Colin Powell.

Any overview of the role of AEI would be remiss without at least a brief mention of John Bolton, the assistant secretary of state for arms control who was imposed on Colin Powell against his will. Bolton used to pull down about $200,000 a year as a vice president at AEI, not bad pay for a job that mostly involves exhaling large quantities of hot air on TV and radio talk shows and writing hackneyed assaults on all things liberal. At State, he has distinguished himself as perhaps the most inept diplomat in the recent history of the department, a liability not only to Colin Powell, but to the United States of America as well.

In the summer of 2001, Bolton led the U.S. delegation to a United Nations meeting aimed at developing a program of action to curb the flow of small arms and light weapons. The idea behind this historic gathering was to develop a global plan to restrict the transfer of the mortars, automatic weapons, and shoulder-fired rockets that are the weapons of choice for the majority of the world's terrorists, thugs, paramilitary forces, and criminal syndicates. One would have thought that at least in this area, even the Bush folks would have seen the value of cooperating with other countries. But one would have been wrong, very, very, wrong.

From the first words to come out of his mouth, Bolton antagonized the vast majority of the assembled diplomats, citizen's groups, and media representatives who had come to the UN meeting on small arms and light weapons. His opening speech was a virtual "ode to the Second Amendment," a long rant on the right of Americans to keep and bear arms that had literally nothing to do with the agenda of the meeting. The target of the UN meeting was weapons of war like the AK-47 assault rifle or the Stinger shoulder-fired missile, not the handguns and hunting rifles that are of concern to the National Rifle Association crowd that forms a staunch pillar of support for the George W. Bush administration. But Bolton ranted on nonetheless, no doubt as a way to show the NRA folks that he was going to "stand up to" the UN and make sure it didn't try to get its hands on "our" handguns and rifles. Bolton even went so far as to name Bob Barr, the Georgia-Republican and NRA board member who was elected to Congress from the district next to Newt Gingrich during the Republican's "class of 1994" landslide in the House of Representatives, to serve as an official observer to the U.S. delegation. Last but not least, Bolton was involved in the decision to kill a proposal by the African delegations that would have added a plank to the UN plan of action on small arms urging governments not to supply arms to non-state groups, whether they were terrorists or self-described "freedom fighters."

Two and one-half years later, with U.S. troops under fire from small arms in Afghanistan, Iraq, and Liberia, Bolton's decision to undermine the UN plan of action on curbing small arms looks particularly ill-advised. But that's okay, he was onto his next diplomatic fiasco—trying to undermine the multi-party talks on capping North Korea's nuclear weapons and missile programs. On the eve of a critical meeting designed to get the talks, which had been allowed to languish—against the advice of Secretary of State Colin Powell—for the first year and one-half of the Bush administration, Bolton delivered an in-your-face, personal attack on North Korean dictator Kim Jong Il. The North Korean regime responded by calling Bolton "scum," and asserting that they would not participate in any talks that he was a part of. It's not news that Kim Jong Il is a major-league bad guy, but the timing of Bolton's outburst, in the midst of a delicate diplomatic opening toward North Korea, could not have been worse. If Colin Powell had free rein to do his job, without worrying about neo-cons trying to force him from office, Bolton would have been fired for insubordination. Instead, in the topsy-turvy world of Bush's Washington, neo-con senator and CSP board member Jon Kyl (R-AZ) launched a broadside against Jack Pritchard, a career military and diplomatic expert who at that point was by far the most experienced person the Bush administration had working the North Korea issue. Pritchard's sin was telling the truth, noting that Bolton's anti-Kim Jong Il outburst on the eve of the talks did not represent the official position of the U.S. government. In the summer of 2003, Pritchard left the Bush administration. He claimed that he was not forced out as a result of the neo-con backlash against him, but that he had decided months earlier to leave because he felt his expertise on the North Korea issue was not being adequately used by the Bush administration. Whatever the precipitating cause was, the fact that Pritchard has left the Bush State Department while Bolton remains is a sad commentary on just how far Bush and his cronies will go in favoring ideology and bluster over experience and competence.

But just as the National Institute for Public Policy complements CSP's right-wing views on nuclear policy, there is an ideologically sympathetic think tank that mirrors CSP's hard-line views on U.S. policy toward the Middle East: the Jewish Institute for National Security Affairs (JINSA). As with NIPP, CSP has significant overlaps with JINSA, most notably in the form of Defense Policy Board member Richard Perle, who serves on advisory panels for both organizations; Undersecretary of Defense for Policy Douglas Feith, who served as chair of the CSP board and a member of JINSA's board before moving over to the Pentagon; Reagan re-tread Jeane Kirkpatrick, who is an advisor to both groups; and JINSA advisory board chairman David Steinmann, who simultaneously serves as a member of CSP's advisory board.[14]

If it's possible, JINSA may be even more aggressive in its advocacy for a policy of permanent war than Frank Gaffney's outfit has been. JINSA advisors like Michael Ledeen, who handled outreach to Israel for the Reagan administration's illegal Iran/Contra arms-for-hostages operation in the 1980s, likes to talk about the coming era of "total war." In its fervent support for hard-line, pro-settlement, anti-Palestinian Likud-style policies in Israel, JINSA has essentially recommended that "regime change" in Iraq should be just the beginning of a cascade of toppling dominoes in the Middle East. If JINSA has its way, the Bush administration will use military means, covert operations, and strong-arm diplomacy to foment "regime changes" not only in Iraq but also in Iran, Syria, Saudi Arabia, and Egypt. Why this policy of rampant interventionism and destabilization would serve the security interests of either the Israeli or American people is a question that JINSA supporters have no good answer for. In their skewed worldview, overthrowing undemocratic Arab regimes is the royal road to democracy—or at least more pliable, pro-U.S. and Israeli-friendly regimes—in the Middle East and Persian Gulf.

It would be comforting to think that JINSA's raving interventionism is just one input among many that Team Bush will consider in crafting a post-Iraq policy for the Middle East. But like CSP, JINSA has influential friends in high places in the Bush administration. Former JINSA advisor Douglas Feith is in charge of the Pentagon-run, privatized occupation of Iraq, and was no doubt responsible for appointing retired Gen. Jay Garner as the initial head of the U.S. occupation. Garner is a former JINSA advisory board member who also has strong ties to the arms industry through his position as a board member of SY Technologies. It may not surprise you to learn that Garner's firm stands to profit from the Bush doctrine of endless interventions through its involvement in missile defense programs such as the Patriot, which has been used in attempts to blunt Iraqi Scud missiles. We should have known from the moment that Feith and Rumsfeld chose Garner that their approach to the Iraqi occupation was going to literally blow up in their faces. Appointing a retired general affiliated with a firm that has profited from U.S. intervention in the Middle East to run post-invasion Iraq was bad enough. But to appoint a retired general and war profiteer who *also* has affiliated himself with an organization like JINSA, which is on record in support of the Israeli occupation of the West Bank and *against* the Oslo Accords, was breathtaking in its stupidity. If the Bush administration had gone out of its way to find the most polarizing figure possible to run the U.S. occupation of Iraq, they couldn't have made a better choice than Jay Garner. Garner has since been supplanted by veteran diplomat Paul Bremer as head of the U.S. occupation, but his fellow JINSA supporter Douglas Feith still holds most of the cards, through the Pentagon's ability to hand out rebuilding contracts and influence which Iraqis get a say in the future of the country's economy and government.[15]

In keeping with its role as a cheerleader for U.S. intervention in the Middle East, JINSA chose to honor Deputy Secretary of Defense Paul Wolfowitz—known as "Wolfowitz of Arabia" by his critics for his obsession with overthrowing Saddam Hussein and promoting his particular vision of "democracy" throughout the region—to receive the 2002 edition of its Henry M. "Scoop" Jackson public service award. The corporate sponsor for the affair was Northrop Grumman, a company that Wolfowitz worked for as a paid consultant prior to joining Rumsfeld's Pentagon.[16] Wolfowitz's Northrop Grumman connection stood him in good stead with the JINSA crowd. JINSA board members Adm. Leon Edney, Adm. David Jeremiah, and Lieut. Gen. Charles May have also worked for Northrop Grumman as either board members or paid consultants.[17] But if you're interested in corporate firepower, the 2002 Jackson awards paled in comparison with the 2001 ceremonies, which honored Secretary of the Air Force James Roche (a former VP at Northrop Grumman), Secretary of the Navy Gordon England (a longtime executive at Lockheed and General Dynamics), and Secretary of the Army Thomas White (formerly of Enron). The corporate sponsor for the 2001 gala was Boeing, and Rudy De Leon, a former top Clinton administration Pentagon official who now runs Boeing's Washington lobbying operation, served as the official host.[18]

What are we to make of this vast interlocking network of ideologues, retired military men, and corporate executives? It's still ideology first, but the corporate connections are a close second in motivating these think tanks and their operatives to seize and sustain their grip on the U.S. government's security policy apparatus. A veteran intelligence analyst put the relationship between greed and ideology in its proper perspective in an interview with Jason Vest for *The Nation* magazine: "Whenever you see someone identified in print or on TV as being with the Center for Security Policy or JINSA championing a position on the grounds of ideology or principle—which they unquestionably are doing with conviction—you are, nonetheless, not informed that they're also providing a sort of cover for other ideologues who just happen to stand to profit from hewing to the Likudnik and Pax Americana lines."[19]

No survey of the role of right-wing think tanks in shaping the Bush administration's foreign and military policies would be complete without mentioning the Project for the New American Century. In many ways, the founding of PNAC in 1997 marked the opening salvo in the formation of the Bush policy of aggressive unilateralism. The signatories of PNAC's founding statement of principles are a rogue's gallery of intransigent hardliners, ranging from Iran-Contra re-tread Eliot Cohen, to ex-Pentagon hawks I. Lewis Libby, Paul Wolfowitz, and Donald Rumsfeld, to neo-con standbys Frank Gaffney, former Reagan drug czar William Bennett, and Norman Podhoretz, to the president's brother and partner in electoral crime, Jeb Bush. Add signatory Dick Cheney to the roster, and you have the bulwarks of the neo-con network that is currently in the driver's seat of the Bush administration's war without end policies all represented in PNAC's founding document.

The PNAC gang were not satisfied to simply endorse general notions of "peace through strength." They wanted to implement a detailed national security policy agenda. To do so, they issued a report entitled "Rebuilding America's Defenses: Strategy, Forces, and Resources for a New Century." The report was written by then PNAC deputy director Thomas Donnelly, who later left the organization for a more lucrative post at weapons contractor Lockheed Martin, before moving through the revolving door again to a post at the American Enteprise Institute. It drew on the thinking of a hard-right panel of experts that included Donald and Robert Kagan, *Weekly Standard* editor William Kristol, RAND operative Abram Shulsky—whose recent claim to fame has been heading up a special group of analysts who have been helping Donald Rumsfeld spin and distort intelligence data to make the case for war in Iraq—Paul Wolfowitz, and I. Lewis Libby (who is now serving as Vice President Dick Cheney's chief of staff).[20] Donnelly promoted the PNAC report at the time as "a useful road map for the nation's immediate and future defense plans," but he could not have known how right he would be. From advocating missile defense, to weapons in space, to the development of "a new family of nuclear weapons designed to address new sets of military requirements," the PNAC "road map" foreshadowed many of the most troubling initiatives that have been undertaken by the Bush foreign policy team. But the bread-and-butter of the PNAC report was a neo-imperial call for an expanded American security perimeter that would be capable of "multiple constabulary missions" aimed at preserving a "Pax Americana" based on a drive to "secure and expand zones of democratic peace, deter [the] rise of [a] new great power competitor, defend key regions (Europe, East Asia, Middle East), and exploit [the] transformation of war."

As Tom Barry and Jim Lobe have pointed out in their excellent summary of PNAC's agenda, the authors of the organization's security blueprint were alert to the benefits for their agenda of a catastrophic attack on the United States, noting that "the process of transformation is likely to be a long one, absent some catastrophic or catalyzing event—like a new Pearl Harbor."[21] For the aggressive unilateralists at PNAC—many of whom are now firmly ensconced in top jobs in the administration of George W.

Bush—the September 11 terror attacks were a political godsend, in that they created a climate of fear and trauma that made it much easier to promote their aggressive, first-strike agenda.

There was no conspiracy relating to 9/11, but there was a great deal of good old-fashioned opportunism and exploitation in the wake of the attacks. The neo-cons seized the political moment to promote their aggressive agenda, and we have been living with the consequences ever since.

— Chapter 6 Notes —

1   Leon V. Sigal, *Hang Separately: Cooperative Security Between the United States and Russia, 1985–1994*, (New York: Century Foundation Press, 2000), p. 120. The Reagan quote is from a speech he gave to the Japanese Diet on November 10, 1983.

2   For an excellent synopsis of the Bush nuclear doctrine, see William M. Arkin, "Secret Plan Outlines the Unthinkable," *Los Angeles Times*, March 10, 2002.

3   The quote is taken from the White House, "Nuclear Posture Review Report," January 8, 2002. Extensive excerpts from the full 65 page report were posted on the web site of GlobalSecurity.org, at *www.globalsecurity.org*. For a synopsis of the plan see Michael R. Gordon, "U.S. Nuclear Plan Sees New Weapons and New Targets," New York Times, March 10, 2002.

4   William M. Arkin, "Secret Plan Outlines the Unthinkable," op. cit.

5   The report can be accessed at the National Institute for Public Policy's web site, at *www.nipp.org*.

6   Colin S. Gray and Keith Payne, "Victory Is Possible," *Foreign Policy*, Summer 1980, pp. 14–27.

7   Panel members involved in the Payne/NIPP study who have influential posts on the Bush foreign policy team include Deputy National Security advisor Stephen Hadley, Condi Rice's right-hand man; Richard Perle protégé Robert Joseph, who works on counterproliferation issues at the National Security Council; and Stephen Cambone, a favorite of Donald Rumsfeld's who has held several key Pentagon posts in the George W. Bush administration. Cambone is well-placed to help implement the NIPP recommendations, having come into the Bush administration after stints as the staff director of the two Rumsfeld commissions, the 1998 panel that hyped the ballistic missile threat to the United States and the 2001 panel on military uses of outer space. Anyone with Rumsfeld's ear, and Rumsfeld's trust, has a huge leg up in this administration.

8   For an excellent overview of plans to expand and modernize the U.S. nuclear weapons complex, see Natural Resources Defense Council, "Faking Restraint: The Bush Administration's Secret Plan for Strengthening U.S. Nuclear Forces," Washington, DC, NRDC, February 13, 2002.

9 See Hartung and Reingold, *About Face*, op. cit., pp. 10–13.

10 Before joining the Bush administration, Beckner was Lockheed Martin's representative in a three company consortium that had the contract to run the United Kingdom's Atomic Weapons Establishment (AWE). See Hartung and Reingold, op. cit., page 14 and Appendix A.

11 See Hartung and Reingold, *About Face*, p. 32. For up-to-the-minute information on who is serving on the advisory boards of CSP and NIPP, consult their web sites at *www.securitypolicy.org* and *www.nipp.org*.

12 See the "About NIPP" section of the organization's web site, at *www.nipp.org*.

13 Albert R. Hunt, "A Loose Cannon," *Wall Street Journal*, April 24, 2003.

14 For an excellent synopsis of the CSP/JINSA connections, and their influence on Bush administration policies, see Jason Vest, "The Men from CSP and JINSA," *The Nation*, September 2, 2002.

15 On Garner and the occupation of Iraq, see two commentaries I wrote for the progressive web site *TomPaine.com*, "Empowering Iraq: The Devil is in the Details," May 5, 2003; and "Imperial Power or Global Partner: The Right Way to Rebuild Iraq," April 8, 2003.

16 See Hartung and Reingold, *About Face*, op. cit., Appendix A.

17 For these JINSA corporate connections and more, see Jason Vest, "The Men From JINSA and CSP," *The Nation*, September 2, 2002.

18 For background on JINSA and the Jackson dinners, consult the organization's web site at *www.jinsa.org*.

19 Jason Vest, "The Men from JINSA and CSP,"op. cit.

20 "Rebuilding America's Defenses: Strategy, Forces and Resources for a New Century," Washington, DC, Project for the New American Century, September 2000.

21 "Security Strategy Foretold," in Tom Barry and Jim Lobe, "The Men Who Stole the Show," Washington, DC, Foreign Policy in Focus, October 2002 (available at *www.fpif.org*). For a more detailed analysis of the role of the neo-cons in shaping Bush policies, see John Feffer, editor, *Power Trip: U.S. Unilateralism and Global Strategy After September 11* (New York: Seven Stories Press, 2003).

How the Big Three Weapons-Makers
Are Cashing In on the War on Terrorism

 **ASIDE FROM FIRMS** like Halliburton, Bechtel, and the Carlyle Group, the biggest corporate beneficiaries of the Bush administration's doctrine of aggressive unilateralism are the "Big Three" weapons makers—Lockheed Martin, Boeing, and Northrop Grumman.

New York Times columnist Paul Krugman was right on target when he suggested that rather than "leave no child behind," the slogan that Bush stole from the liberal Children's Defense Fund while he was running for president, Bush's true motto should be "leave no defense contractor behind."

Boeing and Lockheed Martin's contracts have jumped by billions of dollars annually to service the Bush administration's narrow, militarized approach to fighting terrorism. In contrast, Bush's signature educational reform bill—The Leave No Child Behind Act—is already underfunded by nearly $10 billion *per year*. The assistance originally promised to struggling school districts in inner cities, rural areas, and low- and moderate-income suburbs has long since been swallowed up by war costs and tax cuts.

In fiscal year 2002, the last year for which full statistics are available, Lockheed Martin ($17 billion), Boeing ($16.6 billion), and Northrop Grumman ($7.8 billion) received more than $41 billion in Pentagon contracts. They now get one out of every four dollars the Pentagon doles out for everything from rifles to rockets, MREs (meals-ready-to-eat) to missiles. The Big Three's share of Pentagon research, development, procurement, supply, and service contracts is likely to increase in the years to come, as they use their unprecedented political clout to grab more than their fair share of the military budget pie. This is especially true for Northrop Grumman, which recently acquired TRW, a major military space and Star Wars contractor that had $2 billion in Pentagon contracts in its own right in 2002.

Each of the Big Three is also wired into numerous other sources of federal contracts beyond the Pentagon. The three firms have contracts for everything from airport security and domestic surveillance to a major Lockheed Martin/Northrop Grumman contract to upgrade the weapons and communications systems for the U.S. Coast Guard, which is now part of the newly formed Department of Homeland Security. All three are also major contractors with the National Aeronautics and Space Administration (NASA). Lockheed Martin and Boeing are partners in the U.S. Space Alliance, a NASA-funded effort to privatize the launching of commercial satellites.

Lockheed Martin is also a major contractor for the Department of Energy's National Nuclear Security Administration (NNSA), which is in charge of developing, testing, and producing nuclear weapons for the Pentagon and the military services. Lockheed Martin has a $2 billion-per-year Department of Energy contract to run Sandia National Laboratories, a nuclear weapons design and engineering facility based in Albuquerque, New Mexico. Lockheed Martin also works in partnership with Bechtel to run the Nevada Test Site, where new nuclear weapons are tested either via underground explosions—currently on hold due to U.S. adherence to a long-standing moratorium on nuclear testing—or computer simulations.

All these additional sources of taxpayer money—from the Department of Homeland Security, NASA, and the Department of Energy's nuclear weapons complex, to non-military and space agencies like the Internal Revenue Service that contract with companies like Lockheed Martin for information processing services—mean that the $41 billion that the Big Three are getting from the Pentagon each year is just the down payment on the federal largesse that is being lavished on these firms.

To put this all in some perspective, Lockheed Martin, which receives well in excess of $20 billion per year in total federal contracts, gets more taxpayer money in an average year than is spent on the largest federal welfare program, TANF (Temporary Assistance for Needy Families)—a program that is meant to provide income support to millions of women and children living below the poverty line. This was also true in the Clinton/Gore era, but the margin between Lockheed Martin's corporate welfare and programs like TANF will only expand in the Bush era.

The Big Three are uniquely well-positioned to benefit from the Bush administration's massive military buildup, in significant part due to the Clinton administration's decision to approve and subsidize a huge wave of post–Cold War mergers among military industry firms. Due to pro-merger policies promoted by Clinton's second Defense Secretary, Bill Perry, weapons makers were able to acquire dozens of formerly independent weapons contractors. For example, Lockheed Martin is a merger of Lockheed and Martin Marietta, engineered by former Martin Marietta CEO Norman Augustine, who arranged to have the taxpayers pick up the tab for at least $855 million in consolidation costs related to the merger, ranging from the costs of dismantling and moving equipment to golden parachutes for top executives and board members that cost taxpayers a cool $31 million, including $8.2 million for Augustine himself. One of the more ironic results of this process was that Lamar Alexander, a former Martin Marietta board member who ran for the Republican presidential nomination in 1996 on a platform of taming "big government" and cutting taxes, was on the receiving end of a $236,000 payment from Lockheed Martin to compensate him for the fact that he was forced to step down from the board of the merged company. Just as agricultural subsidies have been used at times to pay off agribusiness corporations for not growing crops, Alexander—who announced his candidacy dressed in a flannel shirt, trying to come across as a regular guy—was essentially paid off for not coming to Lockheed Martin board meetings.

The regulatory change that allowed firms like Lockheed Martin to add merger consolidation costs to their Pentagon contracts was pushed through by William Perry and John Deutch, then top deputies to Clinton's first defense secretary, former Wisconsin Congressman Les Aspin. As Patrick Sloyan of *Newsday* pointed out in a series of articles on the Clinton administration's merger subsidies, both Perry and Deutch had worked as paid consultants to Martin Marietta before coming to the Pentagon, and therefore needed to receive waivers from the normal conflict-of-interest rules to work on an issue that would so obviously benefit their former employer.[1]

The rationale that Perry presented for the mergers was that it was the only way to force the industry to downsize, so that the Pentagon wouldn't be stuck with the tab for extra overhead generated by inefficient firms running half-empty factories. However, other experts, like former Reagan Pentagon official Lawrence J. Korb of the Council on Foreign Relations, asserted that the Pentagon had plenty of leverage to force consolidation without providing additional subsidies to the big weapons-makers. Korb also pointed out that the alleged savings from reduced overhead might never occur, because once merger mania had created a few giant contractors in the place of the dozens that had existed prior to the merger boom, these mega-companies would have even greater leverage to hold up the Pentagon—and the taxpayers—for higher prices on tanks, ships, and planes.

Korb's argument has been borne out by the realities of the costs of major weapons systems. Lockheed Martin's F-22 is coming in at over $200 million a copy—the most expensive fighter plane ever built. Aircraft carriers and attack subs built by subsidiaries of General Dynamics and Northrop Grumman still cost about $2 billion per copy, the equivalent of the entire military budget of some Third World countries.

As Harvey Sapolsky and Eugene Gholz of the Massachusetts Institute for Technology have demonstrated, the Clinton/Gore merger subsidies failed to close down a single major production line for a combat aircraft, or fighting ship, or armored vehicle.[2] The companies were able to use their connections in the Pentagon and on Capitol Hill to keep Cold War relics funded, either through regular appropriations or congressional add-ons that come on top of what the Pentagon has requested. So, while Perry and Clinton may have had good intentions in subsidizing consolidation costs, in reality all they ended up doing was giving extra money to companies like Lockheed Martin and Boeing, which swallowed up its rival McDonnell Douglas during the merger boom.

While companies fared well under the Clinton/Gore

merger subsidy policy, factory workers did not. Rep. Bernie Sanders (I-VT) rightly described the merger payments as "payoffs for layoffs." Companies were basically given an incentive to lay off workers in the name of "efficiency" without being held accountable to pass the resulting savings to the Pentagon. So tens of thousands of workers lost their jobs and the Big Three collected their government subsidies.[3]

Both Bill Perry and John Deutch took jobs on the boards of major defense firms when they left the Clinton Pentagon—Deutch, who had also served as Clinton's CIA Director, took a seat on the board of Raytheon; Perry took seats at both Boeing and United Technologies. Perry also started his very own Carlyle Group-style defense and high-tech investment advisory firm with former Pentagon colleagues like Paul Kaminski.

While it is true that companies like Boeing and Lockheed Martin have produced some of the most effective weapons systems in history, from the Boeing B-52 bomber to the Lockheed Martin F-16 combat aircraft, they generally function best when they have to compete for scarce government dollars while being kept under close scrutiny by independent auditors and technical experts. Under the stewardship of Donald Rumsfeld and George W. Bush, these companies are now being offered more money with less scrutiny.

The Pentagon budget has jumped from $300 billion to $400 billion and beyond in two short years, and the new Department of Homeland Security has additional tens of billions in contracts to tempt the Big Three.

If there is one dirty deal that symbolizes the degree to which the inmates are now running the asylum at the Pentagon, it is the controversial Air Force plan to lease 100 Boeing 767 commercial aircraft and transform them into aerial refueling tankers. The deal is clearly designed to help Boeing cope with twin setbacks—the dip in airline orders since the September 11 attacks, and its October 2001 loss to Lockheed Martin for the lucrative contract to build the Air Force's next-generation combat aircraft, the J-35 Joint Strike Fighter. But as critics like Sen. John McCain (R-AZ), have stated, "this is war profiteering."[4] In fact, the Congressional Budget Office has determined that the funny-money financing of the deal—leasing planes with an option to buy—will cost U.S. taxpayers up to $5 billion more than it would have cost to buy the planes outright.

The deal was created by men like Sen. Ted Stevens (R-AK), who used his clout as chair of the Senate Appropriations Committee to insert an amendment into the Pentagon's budget *requiring* the Air Force to lease 100 Boeing 767s, to be retrofitted for use as aerial refueling tankers; Air Force Secretary James Roche, a former VP at Boeing's sometime partner Northrop Grumman who has been an early and steadfast champion of the lease arrangement; Boeing chief of Washington operations Rudy DeLeon, a former top official in the Clinton Pentagon who helped run interference for the lease deal in the Executive Branch and on Capitol Hill; and Secretary of Defense Donald Rumsfeld, who has given the deal his blessing, supporting one of the costliest corporate welfare schemes in the long, checkered history of U.S. military procurement.

According to an account by Leslie Wayne of the *New York Times*, a central player in the Boeing leasing scam was Darleen Druyun, who served as principal deputy assistant secretary of the Air Force for acquisition and management while the deal was being made. Internal company and Air Force memos released to the public by Sen. McCain in the summer of 2003 reveal that Druyun, while working as a procurement official at the Pentagon, may have passed on confidential information to Boeing about the bid being presented by rival airline manufacturer Airbus. Druyun has since gone onto greener pastures, as deputy general manager for missile defense systems with . . . Boeing! According to Wayne's analysis, if Druyun passed on proprietary information to Boeing, she may be subject to criminal penalties under the federal Trade Secrets Act.[5] McCain's documents also revealed that two members of the Defense Policy Board, retired Navy admiral David Jeremiah and retired Air Force general Ronald Fogelman, were simultaneously working as paid consultants to Boeing, helping pitch the tanker-lease deal to top Pentagon brass.[6]

Darleen Druyun wasn't the only woman fighting the good fight on Boeing's behalf. Washington's two Democratic senators, Maria Cantwell and Patty Murray, have also been staunch supporters of the deal. Boeing is their state's biggest employer, and this contract could create thousands of new jobs at the company's Seattle area facilities.

When the Boeing lease deal was approaching a key milestone in September of 2003, Keith Ashdown of Taxpayers for Common Sense noted that Boeing's home state connection to two Democratic senators—one of whom, Patty Murray, was up for re-election—might be enough to blunt any possibility of generating an anti-lease agreement coalition composed of liberal Democrats, budget hawks of both parties, and anti-pork activists like Sen. McCain. "Our biggest concern in lobbying this issue is that Democrats will vote with helping Patty Murray [in mind] first, instead of thinking what is the best deal for U.S. taxpayers."[7]

Nothing goes far in George Bush's Washington with Democratic support alone. Boeing has worked overtime to make sure the key members of the Republican Congressional leadership are on their side as well. According to the documents released by McCain's office, Boeing made good use of connections in its "other home state," Illinois, to persuade Speaker of the House Dennis Hastert (R-IL) to make its case to the White House. Boeing moved its headquarters to Chicago in the summer of 2001 after setting up a bidding war to see which city and state would offer it the cushiest tax breaks.[8] The fact that House Speaker Hastert was based in Illinois was no doubt part of Boeing's calculation.

Boeing also used the help of Senate Appropriations Committee chairman Ted Stevens (R-AK), a master in the art of backroom budget deals who has brought billions of dollars in defense business to his home state of Alaska, most notably by pressing for the first ground-based prototypes for the Pentagon's missile defense system to be based there. Boeing couldn't offer Stevens much in the way of home state pork out of the lease deal—the planes would be built and refurbished in Seattle, Washington, and Wichita, Kansas, and based in North Dakota, Florida, and Washington state, all home states of key members of the appropriations committee who would need to approve the deal of it was to go forward.[9] But the company could offer Stevens a massive infusion of campaign cash. According to an analysis done by veteran Pentagon-watcher John Donnelly of *Defense Week*, in November 2001—less than a month before Stevens inserted the amendment into the Pentagon budget that instructed the Air Force to lease 100 of the company's 767 aircraft—Boeing threw a fundraiser for Stevens in Seattle at which 32 company executives ponied up a total of $22,000 for Steven's re-election campaign.

This one fundraiser accounted for the bulk of Boeing's $34,000 in contributions to Stevens during the 2002 election cycle, a sum that made the company the Alaska senator's top donor for that period. Boeing executives who wrote checks to Stevens campaign include CEO Phil Condit; Jim Albaugh, the head of the company's Integrated Defense Systems Unit; and Rudy DeLeon, the former Pentagon official who now runs the company's Washington lobbying operation. Even more surprising were the ample donations from executives in Boeing's commercial aircraft division, including Michael Bair, the executive in charge of the company's new 7E7 "Dreamliner" project and Alan Mullally, the head of the company's commercial operations. Most of the executives on the commercial side of the company had no prior history of giving to Stevens, and none of them gave money to any other federal candidate in 2000.[10]

Ken Boehm, director of the National and Legal Policy Center, suggested that "The large contributions to Stevens by Boeing officials in the same time frame as he was pushing the tanker deal certainly has the appearance of impropriety; there is an appearance of a quid pro quo." Eric Miller of the Project on Government Oversight was more blunt: "You would have to be paid off to vote for such a bad deal."[11] As of September 2003, Senate Armed Services Committee Chairman John Warner had thrown a slight wrench in Boeing's plans by pushing through a cap of twenty-five planes, just one-quarter of the number Boeing and the Pentagon were seeking. Warner had two main objections: First, he didn't want to set a precedent for leasing deals of this kind, because they would allow the Pentagon and its contractors to do an end run around normal congressional oversight and budgeting processes. Second, he objected to the fact that the leasing deal involved huge "balloon" payments that would come due eight to ten years down the road, saddling future generations—and future secretaries of defense—with the bill. But for all of his concern, Warner still signed off on a version of the leasing bill, even if it was less than half a loaf from Boeing's perspective.

In July of 2003, Boeing was penalized by the Pentagon for illegally obtaining confidential Lockheed Martin documents that the company used to give it an edge in winning Pentagon satellite contracts. But rather than punishing the company as a whole, the Pentagon only penalized the specific unit of the firm that was involved in the illegal data pilfering, a move that many industry analysts viewed as a slap on the wrist at most. Although the Pentagon did remove Boeing from the running for satellite business worth roughly $1 billion, the company is still receiving its own version of a multi-billion dollar tanker lease deal, plus $986 million in add-ons for projects like the C-17 transport aircraft and the F/A-18E/F fighter plane, which were tucked into the 2003 defense budget by Boeing-friendly legislators like Ted Stevens.

Boeing has provided more than $20 million in capital to Richard Perle's investment firm, Trireme, and gives numerous high-level donations, including $100,000 for George W. Bush's inaugural. The company continues to accumulate influential friends on Capitol Hill by maintaining a steady stream of donations and contracts steered to districts of key members of Congress. Its revolving-door hires of former Pentagon officials like Rudy DeLeon and Darleen Druyun have increased Boeing's insider connections within the Bush administration. In the Bush era, the company has received $16.6 billion in Pentagon contracts in 2002, more than one third more than the $12 billion it received in 2000, the last full year of the Clinton administration.[12]

Boeing's political machinations pale in comparison to the lobbying power of its chief industry rival, Lockheed Martin, which consistently ranks as the Pentagon's top contractor from the mid-1990s to the present. With major facilities in Texas, where the F-16 and F-22 fighters are built, and Georgia, where the C-130 transport plane and parts of the F-22 are constructed, Lockheed Martin is well connected with Congressional Republicans who have strong ties to the Bush White House *and* with conservative southern senators and representatives of both parties who dominate the key committees (like armed services and defense appropriations), who have the most to say about how much the United States spends on specific weapons programs. According to data compiled by the Center for Responsive Politics, Lockheed Martin has been the top political contributor among its military-industrial brethren for the past two election cycles, with $2.4 million in donations in the 2002 cycle and $2.5 million in the presidential election year cycle of 2000. The company accounted for roughly one out of every six dollars of political contributions doled out by weapons contractors in each of those election cycles. If you add the contributions of the other members of the Big Three for 2002, these companies alone made over $4.7 million in political contributions for the cycle, accounting for about one in every three dollars donated by military/aerospace firms.[13]

Lockheed Martin is even more dominant in the area of lobbying expenditures. The firm accounted for $11.7 million of the roughly $60 million in official lobbying expenditures logged by the defense/aerospace sector as a whole in 2000, roughly one out of every five dollars spent.[14] Boeing trailed behind its rival with $7.8 million in lobbying expenditures in 2000, and Northrop Grumman was a close third, spending $6.8 million. The three firms together logged over $26 million for the year, 43 percent of the total lobbying expenditures for the defense sector during the critical presidential election year of 2000.[15]

The defense sector spends more on campaigns than the tobacco lobby, but their political donations pale in comparison with the really big spenders, the finance, insurance, and real estate (FIRE) sector, or the big drug companies. But the Big Three have an advantage that their colleagues in other corporate sectors either lack, or have not been able to exploit to the same degree: fear. They can wrap themselves in the flag, and promise jobs to key congressional and executive branch policy-makers. The jobs come in two forms—at the high end, they hire top policy-makers at lavish sums to help put the squeeze on their former colleagues in government on the company's behalf. At a more mundane level, they can locate weapons factories in the districts and states of key members of Congress in exchange for helping to keep the company's weapons programs funded for as far as the budgetary eye can see.

Lockheed Martin's connections with the Bush family go back to the administration of Bush 41, who engaged in a last-minute-weapons selling binge in the stretch run of the 1992 presidential campaign to show the working men and women of America that he cared about them. As part of this effort, Bush decided to reverse a long-settled American policy of not selling top-of-the-line combat aircraft to Taiwan. He wanted to clear the way for a monster sale of 150 F-16 aircraft to that nation. Two days before the start of the Labor Day weekend, Bush appeared at the Fort Worth, Texas plant where the F-16s are produced to announce the Taiwan sale to a group of cheering, flag waving defense workers. Just to make sure no one missed the point of the exercise, Bush spoke while standing in front of two F-16s, and a banner that said "Jobs for America—Thank You President Bush."[16]

When H. W. Bush approved the Taiwan sale, the F-16 plant was owned by General Dynamics. Lockheed bought it shortly thereafter, and has held on to it ever since as part of their "family of companies," a term its PR flaks were fond of using during its merger frenzy of the 1990s. When Lockheed acquired General Dynamics, it also bought a powerful group of patrons—the Texas Congressional delegation. Members like Rep. Joe Barton (R-TX), whose memo to George Herbert Walker Bush's staffers helped spark the policy reversal that opened the way for the F-16 sale, would now work overtime to help Lockheed Martin keep the Fort Worth F-16 line running. Texas and Georgia representatives would also put their political shoulders into the even more critical task of paving the way for the next plane on the factory's horizon, the F-22 stealth fighter. The F-22 work is split between Fort Worth and Marietta, Georgia, in a factory that is commuting distance from former House Speaker Newt Gingrich's old district.

In addition to running one of the biggest factories in the state during his tenure as governor of Texas, Lockheed Martin had another, more direct link the Bush the younger. While he was governor, the company made an aggressive bid to become the privatized "gatekeeper" for welfare and Medicaid programs in the state of Texas, a policy shift that Bush firmly supported. While they were pursuing the Texas welfare contract, Lockheed Martin hired itself a posse of former Texas legislators and George W. Bush staffers to make its case in Austin, which included Dan Shelley, the guy who had written the provision that allowed for benefits screening in Texas to be put out for bid to private contractors.[17]

However, the company lost its bid to run the Texas welfare system, due to a skillful counter-campaign run by the Texas State Employees Union (TSEU). TSEU ran a series of radio ads that featured the sound of a toilet flushing, followed by a narrator saying "Remember the company that brought you the $3,000 toilet seat? Well now that same company wants to come here and run public services in the State of Texas." The theme of Lockheed Martin as an "outsider," which had only recently bought into the Texas economy, worked well for company opponents. Lockheed Martin lost the contract, which by that time had been reduced to a small pilot project focused on improving the state's data-processing capabilities for dealing with welfare benefits, to a true Texas company, EDS—Ross Perot's former firm.[18]

At the Black Tie and Boots Ball thrown on Bush's behalf during the inaugural festivities in January 2001, Lockheed Martin helped to pay for the party and brought along an F-16 flight simulator which party-goers could jump into if they wanted to play at being a fighter pilot. Once the party was over, Lockheed Martin ensured that, of the thirty-two major Bush administration appointees with direct or indirect links to the arms industry, eight of them came from Lockheed Martin. Officials with indirect ties included Vice President Cheney, whose wife Lynne served on Lockheed

Martin's board from 1994 through January of 2001, stepping down just a few weeks before he took his oath of
office; Deputy National Security Advisor Stephen Hadley,
who worked at the powerhouse DC law firm Shea &
Gardner, which represents Lockheed Martin (along with
numerous other corporate clients); Otto Reich, the right-
wing Cuban-American and Iran/contra re-tread who was
Bush's controversial nominee for Assistant Secretary of
State for Latin American Affairs, who worked as a paid lobbyist for Lockheed Martin when the company was seeking
a reversal of the ban on the sale of high-tech U.S. weaponry to Latin America; and Transportation Secretary Norman
Mineta and his deputy Michael Jackson, both of whom
served as vice-presidents at Lockheed Martin before joining the Bush administration.

The ex-Lockheed Martin employees with the most
direct authority over weapons programs that could benefit
their former company are former company chief operating
officer Peter B. Teets, who was appointed to serve as
Undersecretary of the Air Force and Director of the
National Reconnaissance Office (NRO), a new post creat-
ed by Donald Rumsfeld with an eye towards putting the
responsibility for acquiring military space assets for the
Pentagon under one person's command; and Everet
Beckner, who served as chief executive of Lockheed
Martin's division that helped run the United Kingdom's
Atomic Weapons Establishment (AWE), who was picked to
be Deputy Administrator for Defense Programs at the
Department of Energy's National Nuclear Security

Administration, a post that puts him in charge of supervising his former company's nuclear weapons-related operations at the Sandia National Laboratories in New Mexico and the Nevada Test Site.[18]

While its cultivation and infiltration of the Bush administration is probably unmatched by any other company, Lockheed Martin has not neglected to cultivate key members of Congress as well. The company served as a corporate underwriter for a Trent Lott fundraiser during the run-up to the year 2000 Republican National Convention in Philadelphia, which was billed as the "Lott Hop," because it took the form of a 1950s-style dance party hosted by Dick Clark (yes, *the* Dick Clark of *American Bandstand* fame) featuring music by the Four Tops and Bobby Vee. The event was held at a fieldhouse near the campus of Drexel University, not far from Philadelphia's Union Station. I decided to crash the party and had to stop in the men's room of the train station to wash up, change into a tie and blazer, and buy a few cigars. A journalist friend of mine had suggested that if I was having a hard time getting into the party, I should just offer cigars to the gatekeepers and they would probably let me in. This seemed incredible to me, but I bought the cigars nonetheless, in the hopes that they would serve as some sort of good luck charm.

When push came to shove, I didn't need the cigars. Lott had already spoken to the assembled multitudes, so the crowd was thinning out and they needed more people to fill the room, and to eat the mountains of southern barbecue that were heaped on tables throughout the fieldhouse. The

Four Tops were playing when we entered, and aside from the folks working for the catering company, and one African-American businessman from Lott's home state whose business had been helped along by Brother Lott at some point, the crowd was lily white. The most amazing aspect of the event was the gift bag, which was a yellow and blue cloth tote bag that had the "Lott Hop" logo on one side and a list of corporate sponsors on the other. Lockheed Martin was one of nine corporate entities which ponied up $60,000 each to co-sponsor the event. Other sponsors included the American Gas Association, International Paper, Union Pacific Railroad, the Southern Company ("Energy to Serve Your World"), AT&T, the Bond Market Association, and Freddie Mac ("We Open Doors"), the federally chartered mortgage agency that has since erupted into an Enron-style accounting scandal.

The range of industries involved suggested that Lott's fundraising team may have set up a bidding war to see which company from each industrial sector would have the privilege of bankrolling the event, which was designed both to thank the then senate majority leader's loyal supporters and to fund Lott's "leadership" PAC (Political Action Committee). Lott could then use those funds to make his own contributions to candidates for the House and Senate whose loyalty he wanted to win for future legislative battles.

The funniest element of the gift bag, which included a "Lott Hop" drinking cup and calendar—each with the corporate donors' names splashed liberally upon them—was the commemorative CD, which included the Lott Hop logo and a picture of a young Lott and his partner dancing in a multi-colored spotlight on the front. The CD included classics of the '50s and early '60s like "Under the Boardwalk," "Rockin' Robin," "The Leader of the Pack," "Yakety Yak," and "When a Man Loves a Woman." Aside from "Leader of the Pack," which appeared in its original form, all of the songs had been re-recorded by the original artists specially for the commemorative CD, which was produced by Dominion Entertainment and K-tel Special Products, the same company that used to make those corny compilations that are pitched in late-night TV ads. But the most revealing cut on the CD was the one that was *not* by the artist who originally made it a hit—"Ain't That A Shame," was not presented in the original Fats Domino version, but in a re-recording done by Pat Boone, who next to Trent Lott himself may well be the whitest man in America. The choice of Pat Boone over Fats Domino was ironic given Lott's later troubles over issues of civil rights—triggered by his comment at South Carolina senator Strom Thurmond's memorial service that America would have been a better place if Thurmond's seg-regationist Dixiecrat party ticket had captured the White House in the 1948 elections.

Lockheed Martin didn't limit its support of Lott to sponsoring the "Lott Hop." The company also made regular, large contributions to the Senator's campaign funds, not to mention a $1 million donation to help establish the "Trent Lott Leadership Institute" at the University of Mississippi. And they have received more than their money's worth in return. Lott has been a key player in promoting Lockheed

Martin programs ranging from the C-130 transport plane to the F-22 fighter to the futuristic Space-Based Laser (SBL), which has been lavished with more money than the Pentagon has even asked for due to Lott's insistence. A test facility for the SBL has been placed in the Gulf Coast section of Lott's home state of Mississippi, at the John Stennis Space Center, and Lockheed Martin is playing an integral part in running the facility.

The list of Lockheed Martin's "southern connections"— from its hiring of former Mississippi representative G. V. "Sonny" Montgomery, who used to routinely add a batch of C-130s to the Pentagon budget each year at the company's request, to its revolving-door hire of Buddy Darden, the conservative Democrat from Marietta, Georgia who used to go to bat for the company's C-130 and F-22 aircraft—is long and rich. When he served as Speaker of the House, Newt Gingrich tirelessly lobbied on the company's behalf on Capitol Hill, no doubt because the Marietta plant is within driving distance to Gingrich's suburban Atlanta area district. Former Senate Armed Services Committee Chairman Sam Nunn, a tough, smart guy who generally has his head screwed on straight when it comes to national security policy, was also not above doing a few favors for Lockheed (before its merger with Martin Marietta) on the basis of good old home-state ties.

Mack Mattingly, a former Georgia senator, was hired to head up Lockheed Martin's effort to save the F-22 from the budget cutter's axe back during a spot of trouble a few years back. Unbeknownst to Lockheed Martin, a bipartisan team of Rep. John Murtha (D-PA) and Rep. Jerry Lewis (R-CA, and no relation to the comedian) had decided to put the program's budget on hold due to concerns about cost over-runs and performance problems with the high-priced jet fighter, which was threatening to devour the bulk of the Air Force's procurement budget. With the help of Mattingly and other ex-members of Congress on the Lockheed Martin payroll, the F-22 was placed squarely back onto the Pentagon's budgetary gravy train.

When Mattingly tried for a second go-around as a Georgia senator, running against Democrat Zell Miller, Lott made an appearance on Mattingly's behalf in which he "joked" that if "old Mack" won, he would keep the F-22, but if Miller was reelected, he would move the project to Mississippi. Given Lott's uncanny ability to get plane, ship, and missile defense contracts and deployments targeted on Mississippi, it took some folks a while to realize that he was kidding. Mattingly went down to defeat, but Lockheed Martin has plenty of other allies in the Georgia delegation. In fact, Cynthia McKinney, a progressive Democrat who had a sterling record of standing up to special interests during her tenure as a rep-resentative from Georgia, quickly realized that it was assumed that she would join the other members of the dele-gation in going to bat for the C-130, the F-22, and other Lockheed Martin projects. When she refused to do so, many of her Georgia colleagues—of both parties—were shocked that she would put principle before pork barrel politics.

Like Trent Lott's choice of Pat Boone over Fats Domino, Lockheed Martin's choice of a new slogan may reveal more than it was intended to do. The company recently discarded its old slogan, "Mission Success," in favor of "We Never Forget Who We're Working For." Perhaps the company's PR team abandoned the "Mission Success" mantra because the company had had so many high-profile *failures* in the 1990s, from rigged missile defense tests to misguided launch vehicles that blew up billion-dollar spy satellites before they got anywhere close to being in orbit. Besides, the company has its hand in so many tills—from the Pentagon, to the Coast Guard, to the Department of Energy, to the IRS, to the Postal Service, to state and local governments from Washington, DC to the Hague in the Netherlands—that they probably *frequently* forget who they're working for, and may *need* the new slogan to remind them to pay attention to where the checks are coming from.

Northrop Grumman, the final part of the Big Three, is a hungry conglomerate on the make, hoping to knock Lockheed Martin out of its number one-spot in defense contractor heaven. Their new slogan is "We Define the Future." This doctrine is reflected by their presence in so many cutting-edge new programs, from the Global Hawk unmanned aerial vehicle that saw heavy duty in Afghanistan and Iraq, to the next generation of combat ships (designed by its Newport News shipbuilding unit, a recent acquisition), to its strong presence in the burgeoning field of defense electronics where it makes everything from targeting and reconnaissance systems to major elements of the Bush administration's multi-tiered missile defense program (via its latest acquisition, TRW). Northrop Grumman will also profit handsomely from the U.S. occupation of Iraq through its ownership of the Vinnell Corporation, a private military company which has landed the contract to train the new Iraqi army.[20] Like Lockheed Martin, Northrop Grumman—a company which its critics refer to as "NG," as in "no good"—has alumni sprinkled throughout the Bush administration, from Bush's first secretary of the Air Force, James Roche, to Air Force comptroller Nelson Gibbs, to folks like deputy defense secretary Paul Wolfowitz, who did some consulting for good old "NG" before joining Team Bush.

In a period of ever-expanding military budgets, the Big Three continue to appropriate funds that could be used for education, environmental protection, health care, and to build the nonmilitary industries that are needed to create the well-paying jobs of the future.

We need to take our country back, not simply from the Bush junta, but from the corporate profiteers who all too often have the leaders of both major parties in the palms of their hands.

— Chapter 7 Notes —

1   For a detailed accounting of the merger subsidies and Perry and Deutch's roles in promoting them, see Patrick J. Sloyan, "Sweet Deal from Pentagon: Top Brass OK $60 Million Break to Ex-Employer, Martin Marietta," *Newsday*, June 30, 1994; and William D. Hartung, "Saint Augustine's Rules: Norman Augustine and the Future of the American Defense Industry," *World Policy Journal*, Summer 1996, pp. 64-73.

2   See Harvey Sapolsky and Eugene Gholz, "Private Arsenals: America's Post-Cold War Burden," in Ann Markusen and Sean S. Costigan, editors, *Arming the Future: A Defense Industry for the 21ˢᵗ Century* (New York: Council on Foreign Relations, 1999).

3   On Alexander and the "payoffs for layoffs" scam, see William D. Hartung, "Welfare Kings," *The Nation*, June 19, 1995. And for an overview of the military-industrial influence peddling that went on in the Clinton era, see William D. Hartung, "Military Industrial Complex Revisited: How Weapons Makers are Shaping U.S. Foreign and Military Policies," in Martha Honey and Tom Barry, editors, *Global Focus: U.S. Foreign Policy at the Turn of the Millennium* (New York: St. Martin's Press, 2000), pp. 21–43. The chapter is also available on the web in the form of a Foreign Policy in Focus special report, at *www.foreignpolicy-infocus.org/papers/micr/index.html*.

4   Statement of Sen. John McCain on the floor of the U.S. Senate, December 20, 2001. Copies of recent statements by McCain on military waste, fraud, and abuse are available on his web site, at *http://mccain.senate.gov*.

5   Leslie Wayne, "Documents Show Extent of Lobbying by Boeing," *New York Times*, September 3, 2003.

6   Anne Marie Squeo, "Air Force Ex-official Had Tics To Boeing During Contract Talks," *Wall Street Journal*, October 7, 2003.

7   Katherine Pfleger, "Tanker Critics, Backers Ready for Showdown in U.S. Senate," *Seattle Times*, September 3, 2003.

8   On Boeing's Chicago deal, see Amity Shlaes, "Big State Spending that Brings Small Rewards: Boeing Has Been Promised Dollars 60m To Site Its Headquarters in Illinois. The Deal Looks a Poor One for Taxpayers," *Financial Times* (London), May 15, 2001.

9   John Donnelly, "Boeing Payments to Senator Raise Questions,"

Defense Week, September 2, 2003. References to Boeing donations to Stevens in the rest of this section are based on this article as well.

10 Donnelly, "Payments to Senator Raise Questions," op. cit.

11 Quotes are from Donnelly, op. cit.

12 For a capsule summary of how the Big Three defense contractors and their smaller brethren have profited from the Bush administration's defense policies, see Ceara Donnelley and William D. Hartung, "New Numbers: The Price of Freedom in Iraq and Power in Washington," a World Policy Institute special report available at *www.worldpolicy/projects/arms*, under "reports."

13 Contributions data are from the Center for Responsive Politics Open Secrets data base on campaign spending, which is accessible at *www.opensecrets.org*.

14 The year 2000 is the most recent year for which full lobbying statistics are available. For updates on lobbying and campaign spending by major corporations and individuals, consult the Center for Responsive Politics web site, cited above.

15 Lobbying figures are also from the Open Secrets data base, cited above.

16 The full story of Bush's arms sales binge during the stretch run of the 1992 presidential campaign can be found in William D. Hartung, *And Weapons for All* (New York: HarperCollins, 1995), pp. 276-285. See also Lee Feinstein, "Administration to Sell Advanced Fighters to Taiwan," *Arms Control Today*, September 1992; and Michael Wines, "$8 Billion Directed to Wheat Farmers and Arms Workers," *New York Times*, September 3, 1992.

17 On Lockheed Martin's use of revolving door hires in pursuit of the Texas welfare contract, see Suzanne Gamboa, "State Contract Lobby Efforts Raise Concern," *Austin American-Statesman*, July 6, 1996, and Polly Ross Hughes, "Bush's Ex-Aide Now Lobbyist For Firm Bidding To Run Welfare," *Houston Chronicle*, March 18, 1997.

18 For more of the sordid details of Lockheed Martin's pursuit of welfare-to-work contracts in Texas, California, Florida and beyond, see William D. Hartung and Jennifer Washburn, "Lockheed Martin: From Warfare to Welfare," *The Nation*, March 2, 1998.

19 The information on the Bush administration's hiring of defense industry officials in general and Lockheed Martin officials in particular comes from William D. Hartung and Jonathan

Reingold, "About Face: The Role of the Arms Lobby in the Bush Administration's Radical Reversal of Two Decades o U.S. Nuclear Policy," New York, World Policy Institute, May 2002, pp. 13-16, and Appendix A. The report, which drew heavily on the fine work on this subject done by the Center for Public Integrity, can be accessed on the Institute's web site at *www.worldpolicy.org/projects/arms*, under "reports."

[20]For more on Vinnell, see William D. Hartung, "Bombings Bring U.S. 'Executive Mercenaries' Into the Light," *Los Angeles Times*, May 16, 2003.

Taking Our Country Back: A Question of Balance

"We face a hostile ideology—global in scope . . . ruthless in purpose, and insidious in method . . . [T]he danger it poses promises to be of indefinite duration. To meet it successfully, there is called for, not so much the emotional and transitory sacrifices of crisis, but rather those which enable us to carry forward steadily, surely, and without complaint the burdens of a prolonged and complex struggle—with liberty the stake."

—President Dwight D. Eisenhower, farewell radio and television address to the American people, January 17, 1961

"We are now faced with the fact that tomorrow is today. We are confronted with the fierce urgency of now."

—Dr. Martin Luther King, Jr., A Time to Break Silence Address to Clergy and Laity Concerned, Riverside Church, New York, NY, April 4, 1967

"The problem is not in our stars, but in ourselves."

—William Shakespeare, *Julius Caesar*

 **I BEGIN AND END** this book with quotes from Dwight Eisenhower and Martin Luther King, Jr., for a reason. Both men spoke the truth to power at moments of genuine national emergency, and both of them have messages that resonate today.

The years immediately following Eisenhower's warning, marked by the Cuban Missile Crisis and the beginnings of the escalation of America's intervention in Vietnam, were among the most perilous in the history of our Republic. As former Kennedy aide Ted Sorensen has pointed out, if our young president had not had the courage and confidence to overrule the hard-liners who wanted to go to war over the issue of Soviet missiles in Cuba, we might well have witnessed a nuclear confrontation between Washington and Moscow. Thankfully, at a time of great danger, cooler heads prevailed.

If a similar crisis occurred today, would George W. Bush have the presence of mind to overrule right-wing ideologues like Richard Perle, Donald Rumsfeld, and Paul Wolfowitz in a confrontation with a nuclear-armed North Korea, or an unexpected showdown with China? Maybe yes, maybe no. But I for one would be far more comfortable with a more mature, less aggressively self-righteous leader with his finger on the nuclear button. And I would like to have a president who gives greater weight to the opinions of career professionals in the military, intelligence, and foreign service communities than he does to the ravings of self-serving ideologues like Don Rumsfeld and his band of yes-men at the Pentagon. Given Bush's conduct thus far in his self-declared "war on terrorism," that may be too much to expect.

Coming from very different backgrounds and perspectives, both President Eisenhower and Dr. King were sounding an alarm about the need to protect, defend, and revitalize our democracy. When King spoke out against the Vietnam War on the evening of April 4, 1967, he could not have known that he would be taken from us exactly one year later by an assassin's bullet. His call to recognize the "fierce urgency of now"—and to act accordingly—is even more relevant today than it was a quarter of a century ago when he first uttered those words.

We need to act now because we are dealing with a ruling group that is more concerned with consolidating its own power than it is with protecting and defending our Constitution. Let's not forget that this is a president who had no qualms about building a case for war against Iraq based on phony claims about Saddam Hussein's nuclear, chemical, and biological weapons capabilities and bogus assertions about an operational link between Saddam Hussein and Osama Bin Laden. Whether President Bush lied through his teeth, or was merely misled by his advisors, is immaterial. At a time of great national vulnerability, we have a commander-in-chief who puts greater stock in right-wing fantasies about how the world works than he does in careful analysis of the threats we face as a nation.

Our current debacle in Iraq is just the beginning of the troubles that this obscenely irresponsible approach to national security policy may bring down on our nation if all of us don't stand up and say no. No, this is not what we signed up for. No, this is not the kind of country we want to live in. No, we do not want the United States to act like the bull in the global china shop, poised to bust up the place on the slightest provocation but incapable of putting things back together again once we have lashed out at our enemies, real or imagined.

Before I go into detail about what you can and should be doing to help take our country back from the Bush/Cheney/Rumsfeld/Ashcroft "axis of irresponsibility," it's worth reflecting a bit on the quote from President Eisenhower that started off this chapter. It is not one of the better known passages of his military-industrial complex speech, but it may be the one with the most direct relevance to the position we find ourselves in today.

Being a man of the '50s, the "relentless adversary" that Eisenhower was referring to was of course Communism, with a capital "C." I don't necessarily share his views on the scope of that threat, but that's not what matters for our purposes here. Given how central, and how menacing, and how tenacious he felt the Soviet threat was, it's fascinating to contemplate how *measured* he felt that our national response should be. Eisenhower was basically saying that no matter how frightening or brutal our enemy of the moment is, we shouldn't freak out, and we shouldn't go off on some sort of unsustainable "crash program" to deal with it. Most importantly of all, Eisenhower argued that *we shouldn't undermine our liberties in the name of national defense.*

Today, when our nation faces a very different kind of "relentless adversary"—catastrophic terrorism of global reach fueled by a perverted version of fundamentalist Islam—Eisenhower's suggestion that we "carry forward steadily, surely, and without complaint" is more important than ever. Unfortunately, Eisenhower's advocacy of a balanced approach is the polar opposite of what the Bush/Cheney/Rumsfeld gang have chosen to do. In the months and years since the September 11 attacks, our leadership in Washington has thrown hundreds of billions of dollars at the Pentagon, run up record budget deficits, and undermined basic civil liberties, all in the name of fighting terrorism. This is not the measured, balanced response Eisenhower would have recommended. This is a government shifting into overdrive, taking desperate measures that may well end up destroying our democracy in order to save it.

Not only is the Bush administration's approach to fighting terrorism unsustainable, it is also profoundly unworkable. We have used nineteenth-century tools—military intervention and conquest—to fight a twenty-first-century adversary. Our enemy, the Al Qaeda terror network, is a small, disciplined, stealthy organization with a presence in as many as sixty countries. Osama Bin Laden is a terrorist leader, but he is also a global businessman who at various times has owned or controlled construction businesses, honey shops, and illicit diamond and arms trading networks. Unlike during the Cold War, when rebels, revolutionaries, and thugs of all political stripes often relied on government sponsors for guns and money, Al Qaeda has exploited the mechanisms of our global economic system and found a way to sustain itself with or without the support of government sponsors.

Bush and company can overthrow all the governments they want to, but they will not *necessarily* eliminate the ability of Al Qaeda and its allies to carry off additional mass casualty terror attacks against the United States, its military forces, and its friends around the world. And given how much money they are blowing on their ill-fated occupation of Iraq, they may not be able to *afford* too many more "regime changes," even if their spirits are willing. Take the case of Iraq, where U.S. troops have become a big fat target for every terrorist, crank, and malcontent in the Middle East and South Asia to take pot shots at. In this seminal example, it seems clear that the Bush doctrine of "preventive war," first strikes, and regime change is *increasing* the ability of terrorists to strike at Americans, not decreasing it. And the more troops, the more intelligence operatives, and the more resources we pour into Iraq, the less we have left for the battle against Al Qaeda, a battle which has very little to do with the fate of Saddam Hussein.

The question is, are Bush and company simply misguided in their approach to fighting terrorism, or are they pursuing a different agenda altogether? Are they primarily concerned with making the average American safer, or are they primarily concerned with creating a position of U.S. military, political, and economic dominance that serves the interests of a small ideological, political, and economic elite in this country?

My sense is that they are trying to do both. The problem we face is that Bush and his key advisors actually seem to *believe* that their approach—a policy of talking loudly and arrogantly and carrying a big stick—represents the one true path to global security, prosperity, and freedom. Because they are true believers, they are able to project an aura of confidence even as their grand plan for global domination seems to be crashing down around their ears.

All you have to do is listen to Donald Rumsfeld talking about how things are getting better and better in Iraq, every day in every way, to understand how the ideology of Bush's key advisors allows them to float above the unpleasant consequences of their actions.

The Bush crowd can't be reasoned with. All we can do is take their power away, as quickly and efficiently as possible. That's where you come in.

As we compare the Bush administration's rhetoric about creating a "democracy" in Iraq with the realities on the ground there, we should also take a few moments to take stock of the state of our democracy here in America. There is a link between what's happening in Baghdad and what's going on in Washington that may help us understand a bit more about how to drive Bush and company from power.

In Iraq, the Pentagon is running the show, promoting a small group of handpicked Iraqis like Ahmed Chalabi to serve as the core of a new, "democratic" government. Many of the key figures that Rumsfeld, Paul Wolfowitz, and

Douglas Feith have been promoting to positions of power in the interim Iraqi governing council—and, hopefully, from their perspective, in the government that finally takes charge in Iraq—were literally on the Pentagon's payroll prior to the U.S. invasion. In early 2003, well before the U.S. intervention, a group of roughly 150 Iraqi exiles were working at the defense contractor SAIC, biding their time until they could be dropped into key positions of power in U.S.-run ministries in "liberated Iraq." Pentagon officials acknowledged that they put them to work at SAIC rather than inside the Pentagon itself primarily for PR purposes, so they would not have Pentagon phone numbers. Since the occupation has begun, even a number of the Pentagon's handpicked Iraqi "leaders" have complained bitterly that their suggestions are being ignored, that they are not in the room when the real decisions are being made, and that they are in effect figureheads.

In the meantime, the Bush administration's privatized approach to rebuilding Iraq, which activist groups like Global Exchange and the Institute for Southern Studies have called the "second invasion"—the *corporate* invasion—of Iraq, is proceeding apace.[3]

Even if Iraq does by some miracle move beyond the Pentagon's handpicked puppets to a genuinely representative government, many of the key decisions about how to run the country will have already been made. Dyncorps, the U.S. firm that caused a scandal in the Balkans when two of its employees were caught running a child prostitution ring, has a contract to train personnel for a new Iraqi justice system. Vinnell, a subsidiary of Northrop Grumman that has come under fire for its controversial role in training the Saudi royal family's personal protection service, the Saudi National Guard, has a contract to train the members of the new Iraqi armed forces. Philip Carroll, the former chief executive of Royal/Dutch Shell, was chosen as the first U.S. overseer of the new Iraqi oil ministry, and new contracts have already been issued to supply Iraqi oil not only to Carroll's former company, but to Chevron, the firm that named a tanker after Condoleezza Rice after her stint as a member of their board of directors. We've already discussed the central role of Halliburton in the rebuilding and operation of Iraq's oil infrastructure. And don't forget Bechtel, which has a contract for $680 million and counting to rebuild basic roads and buildings in Iraq.

Congressional scrutiny of the Bush administration's $87 billion emergency spending package to sustain the U.S. occupation in Iraq and the U.S. intervention in Afghanistan has turned up billions of dollars in gold-plated activities that are tailor made for generating new contracts for Halliburton, Bechtel, Dyncorps, and other politically-connected companies and consultants. The Bush administration's Iraq supplemental is replete with opportunities to throw more money at its favorite companies and consultants, all in the name of "rebuilding Iraq." Major expenditures include $100 million for building seven "model communities" complete with houses, schools, roads, and clinics; $400 million to build two 4,000-bed prisons; and another $100 million to hire 100 experts at $100,000 each over a six-month period to assist in prison reconstruction. These rebuilding items are just the tip of the iceberg. There are hundreds of millions, if not billions, in additional funds for rebuilding Iraq's oil infrastructure, money that will go straight to Vice President Cheney's former firm, Halliburton. And don't forget that much of the money reserved for training new Iraqi military and police forces will go to U.S. contractors like DynCorp and Vinnell.[4]

Even the Bush administration's half-hearted efforts to "open up" the rebuilding process in Iraq to competitive bidding seem to be designed to help the usual suspects. While much was made of Bush's October 2003 decision to put Condoleezza Rice and the National Security Council in charge of a series of working groups that would coordinate U.S. policy in Iraq and Afghanistan, few analysts noticed that the Pentagon was simultaneously being handed *more power* to control the contracts that will be handed out for the rebuilding of Iraq.[5] Meanwhile, the revolving door keeps spinning around. As this book went to press, it was announced that Joe Allbaugh, the former director of the Federal Emergency Management Agency (FEMA)—who also served as George W. Bush's campaign manager in the controversial 2000 presidential elections—was starting a consulting firm called New Bridge Strategies, whose sole purpose for existing is to help other companies cash in on the rebuilding of Iraq.[6]

And despite the promises of fair and open competition by the U.S.–run Coalition Provisional Authority (CPA), a mid-October account by the *New York Times* suggests that its still the usual suspects who are likely to get the vast bulk of the contracts in Iraq: early tenders from the CPA called for suppliers to supply finished bids within as little as three days, a virtually impossible task for a company that hadn't already been doing business with the U.S.–run Iraqi governing authority.[7] Those companies that do break into the small circle of privileged contractors will no doubt do so by hiring someone like Joe Allbaugh who has friends in high places, a guy who can make the right calls, and open the right doors, at the right time . . . for a fee of course.

So, let's see—a handpicked regime which spends most of its time giving out contracts and other favors to its corporate friends. That's a fair description of what's happening in Iraq, all in the name of democracy, George W. Bush style. But isn't that also a fair description of what's happening in America? We have a president who was selected for office by a partisan majority on the Supreme Court, despite the fact that his opponent received more votes, not only nationwide, but even in Florida, the decisive state in terms of winning the majority of votes in the electoral college. He and his party have done everything they can since that moment to consolidate their power, from supporting partisan, pro-Republican redistricting plans in key states to using the power and resources of the presidency for repeated visits to swing states, bearing gifts. As in Iraq, in the U.S. context the Bush team has a penchant for giving preferential treatment to companies whose executives support the Republican agenda (or at least give large sums to Republican candidates, whatever they may think of the Bush crowd).

The Bush gang is perfectly willing to distort the truth to

keep its grip on all three branches of government, and to use surrogates in the Congress and pro-Republican media outlets like Fox News and Clear Channel Communications—a communications giant that owns 1,200 radio stations nation-wide—to amplify its message. Fox News is run by Roger Ailes, a former Reagan political operative who thinks nothing of coordinating his "news coverage" with the needs of an incumbent Republican president. And Clear Channel's vice chairman is Tom Hicks, a longtime Bush family friend and former business partner of George W. Bush's who helped him buy an ownership stake in the Texas Rangers baseball team while putting virtually no money down.[5]

As you have no doubt noticed, the president and his surrogates think nothing of smearing their political opponents as being "soft on terrorism." They have no qualms about continuing to promote demonstrably false charges like Vice President Dick Cheney's September 2003 allegation regarding a meeting between an Al Qaeda operative and a representative of Saddam Hussein's government in Prague, a meeting which professional intelligence sources in the United States, Britain, and the Czech Republic all say never happened.

To a remarkable degree, the Bush propaganda campaign is still working, even as their policies are falling to shreds in their hands. As this book went to press, nearly seventy per-cent of Americans believed that Saddam Hussein played a role in the September 11 terror attacks, a demonstrably false assertion that no responsible analyst either in or out of the United States government believes to be true.

Amazingly enough, the number of Americans believing this *increased* during a period in which the mainstream media was running regular reports about the degree to which the Bush administration's case for war in Iraq had been based on distortions and shoddy evidence. This is no doubt because Bush and his key aides use spin and body language to insinuate a connection between Saddam Hussein and Al Qaeda at every opportunity.

If the Bush folks don't dazzle you with their PR, they can always try to scare you into submission. Under the leadership of John Ashcroft, the Bush administration has increased government surveillance of ordinary citizens. They have also promoted arbitrary arrests and detentions, of immigrants and citizens alike, who are often denied such basic rights as access to an attorney or a presentation of the charges against them for weeks or months at a time.

To recap, we have a president who was selected under questionable circumstances, who has used the power of his office and his right-wing network in the media and think tank worlds to advance the partisan and financial interests of his cronies. He has also undermined our basic freedoms in the name of fighting terrorism. It would be a vast exaggeration to say that our democracy is in as sorry a shape as the pale reflection of a representative republic that Rumsfeld and company are building in Iraq. But it *is* fair to say that during George W. Bush's term, our democratic freedoms have been diminished, while the power of wealthy individuals and corporations has been enhanced. That's why we need to be at *least* as concerned with the future of democracy in *America* as we are with the future of democracy in Iraq.

Eisenhower had it right—we need to defend ourselves, but we need to do it in a way that is sustainable, and that doesn't undermine our basic liberties. George W. Bush doesn't grasp that, in large part because he has such a diminished understanding of what terms like "democracy" and "liberty" really mean. Things have come relatively easily to him in his life and career, and he doesn't seem to understand that entire generations of Americans fought and died, both at home and abroad, to preserve and expand our democracy. Our hard-won democratic rights are not something that any president should take lightly, much less sacrifice to some allegedly higher purpose or goal. George W. Bush doesn't realize that, and that's why he's not fit to be the president of this republic at this crucial moment in our history.

We've looked at the Bush crowd and what makes them tick. Now we need to get down to the serious question of what we're going to do to get their hands off of the levers of power in our country. That's where you come in. It's time to stop treating our democracy like a spectator sport, and start reminding ourselves of our responsibilities as citizens. It's time to stop whining, put down the remote, and start taking concrete actions to drive Bush and his whole gang of ideologues and scam artists out of Washington.

When I first started out in my current line of work in the late 1970s and early 1980s, I used to give long, elaborate speeches about the power of the arms lobby. When I got done, people generally had one of two reactions. They would either say something like, "God, Bill, that's terrible—what are *you* planning to do about it?" Or, they would say, "Wow, the other side is even more powerful than I thought—we're *never* going to beat these guys." Needless to say, neither of these responses were what I was looking for. I wanted to inspire people to take action against the distortions of our foreign policy, our federal budget, and our purposes as a nation that were being carried out in the name of national security. I obviously needed a new game plan.

What I've learned since my early forays into public speaking is that you need to give your audience some hope that they can have an impact on the problems you are presenting to them. You need to give one part information, one part inspiration, and one part recommendation of concrete steps. That's what I'm going to do with you, right now. I don't want you to go away from this book informed, or outraged, or disappointed, or intrigued—I want you to go away from this book with a commitment to *doing something concrete* to help change the course of this country. Otherwise, we could have just as easily spent the time that it took to write—and to read—this book sipping martinis, or hanging out at the beach, or reading trashy novels. These are all things that you are welcome to do, by the way, as long as you *also* spend some time every day trying to change the minds of your friends, neighbors, and fellow Americans. At a time like this, citizenship is an obligation, not an optional activity. So let's see what you can do to make the world a better place for yourself, your family, and the generations yet to come.

I recommend starting small—unless you are already

knee-deep into working on these issues, in which case, keep up the good work! Balance and sustainability are the key points here. Everyone I know is already stressed to the max with their jobs (or lack thereof), their kid's school, or bread-and-butter issues affecting their local community, from crime to traffic safety to striving to maintain a healthy environment. So, who has the time to worry about the 2004 elections, or how best to protect our nation, or all the other big picture issues I have raised in this book?

You do. But as I said, you can start slowly and build up as your time, interests and energy permit. Here are a few simple themes around which to structure your own "action plan" for helping take back our country.

Promote Political Literacy

If you're the kind of person who spends fifteen minutes a day or more ranting about how screwed up things are, or yelling at the TV screen, or otherwise complaining about the state of our world and our nation, you need to refocus that energy toward something constructive. One good place to start is by educating yourself and your fellow citizens about what's actually going on in the world. In this age of the Internet, you have no excuse not to be well informed. No matter how much crap they put on *Fox TV* or the nightly network news programs, you can make yourself better informed than the average TV news anchor in fifteen minutes to half an hour a day.

There are plenty of ways to use the Web to improve your political literacy, and I will just mention a few that have worked for me. One great thing to do is to set your home page on your computer to an independent news site like *Commondreams.org*, *AlterNet.org*, *TomPaine.com*, or *TheNation.com*. That way, every time you log on you will have the opportunity to quickly read an article or two of in-depth analysis or commentary on a serious issue of domestic or foreign policy that you will *never* learn about on television, and which may not make it into your local paper. Most of these sites are set up so that you can easily forward these articles to friends, if you feel they contain something they *must* know about.

You can also generally get on a list-serve to receive regular updates from an independent news source like *The Nation* or *TomPaine.com*.

The key here is managing your time. You could obviously spend hours on end reading really interesting stuff on the Web, but if you don't put that information to good use, it won't help matters much. So whether you get on a list-serve, or decide to read a given newspaper or magazine online—be it the British *Guardian*, or the *Washington Post*, or *Salon.com*—make sure you share what you learn with others, and try to encourage them to tap into a more sophisticated flow of commentary and analysis than they will get by being passive consumers of TV news.

In an ideal world, we would have a diverse, decentralized mass media that presented critical views of the government as a central part of its mission. One day, perhaps we will have such a media. But for now, the best alternative to that is to reorganize the way we interact with the media, by becoming active seekers of high quality, independent information. Just as a country that can't teach its kids to read has a grim economic future, a country that can't get its citizens to take greater responsibility for achieving a more sophisticated understanding of the world around them has a grim political future. It's up to us to educate ourselves and our fellow citizens for the political battles to come.

Act in Concert with Others

Whatever you decide to do with what you've learned, it will be more powerful if you do it in cooperation with your fellow citizens. Your options for cooperative action range from joining your local chapter of Peace Action (*www.peace-action.org*), the nation's largest grassroots peace and justice organization, to getting on the list of Moveon.org.

Moveon.org is a Web-based activist network that has done amazing things by mobilizing its one-million-plus member list to do everything from supporting peace candidates to financing issue ads in the *New York Times*, to bombarding Congress with antiwar letters, faxes, and e-mails. They have started a site called *Misleader.org*, which provides a compendium of misstatements by President Bush that can be accessed on the Web, or by signing up for regular e-mail updates.

Three other organizations worth working with if you have a little bit of time to spend each day are Win Without War (*www.winwithoutwarus.org*), True Majority (*www.truemajority.org*), or 20/20 Vision (*www.20/20vision.org*). Win Without War is a coalition of forty national organizations whose founding premise is "advocating alternatives to preemptive war against Iraq to keep America safe." Members of Win Without War include the American Friends Service Committee, Business Leaders for Sensible Priorities, the NAACP, the National Council of Churches, the National Organization of Women, Veterans for Common Sense, and Women's Action for New Directions. As this went to press, Win Without War had launched a "Change the Team" campaign calling for, among other things, the resignation of Donald Rumsfeld. True Majority ("Give us two minutes a month. We'll give you a better world.") sends out two action-oriented e-mails per month on issues ripe for congressional action. 20/20 Vision ("Busy people taking action for peace and the environment") sends out regular action alerts on breaking issues. If you go to their Web site you will see a brief synopsis of each of their current issues, and if you are moved to act you can enter your zip code and address and move to a screen where you can send a letter or e-mail to your member of Congress (since the anthrax scare, a lot of members are accepting e-mail only—20/20 Vision's Web site will tell you if that's the case for your representative). Hooking up with any one of these three, or with Moveon.org, would give you a way to weigh in regularly on important issues with a small investment of your time— probably more than the two minutes promised by True Majority, but possibly a half hour or less *per month*.

Finding the right level of activism is a matter of taste. If you don't want to be pinned down to regular meetings or tasks, you can always check in periodically at a the Web site of United for Peace and Justice (*www.unitedforpeace.org*), the national coalition that helped organize the massive peace marches in the United States and around the world in February and March of 2003. They have a full list of upcoming activities, listed nationally, regionally, and locally. You can plug in as time permits, or help organize an action in your area.

Keep Hope Alive

On June 12, 2002, I participated in a celebration of the twentieth anniversary of the June 12, 1982 nuclear disarmament march that brought one million people to New York's Central Park. It was cosponsored by the Nation Institute and the New York State chapter of Peace Action. In the run-up to the event, the organizers decided to move the venue from a church that held 1,000 to 1,200 people to the New York Ethical Culture Society auditorium, which holds about 600 to 700. The reason—we didn't want the group to look too small if we drew a few hundred folks in a place that could hold a thousand or more.

Going from one million marchers in 1982 to a few hundred audience members in 2002 seemed like a big falling off of interest in the issue, and in some ways it was. But what we didn't realize that night was that we were meeting at a time when the global peace movement was about to enter an extraordinary period of growth. By June of 2003, just one year after our hearty hundreds gathered at the New York Ethical Culture Society to keep the flame of disarmament flickering, New Yorkers had organized two major peace demonstrations of 300,000 to 500,000 each, one *before* the Bush administration intervened in Iraq, and one a few days after the start of the war. And we were not alone. There were scores of similar demonstrations being held across the United States and around the world, in what we now know were the largest coordinated global peace demonstrations in history.

We didn't stop the war, but we did build a movement of unprecedented size, scope, and diversity. We need to channel some of that same energy into sending Bush, Cheney, and Rumsfeld packing after November 2004. This is no time to get discouraged.

No one *really* expected Team Bush to see the error of its ways. But if we can get the millions who marched to also vote, and encourage their friends and relatives to vote, we can win the battle that counts, the battle of the ballot box.

Make Your Words, and Your Dollars, Count

Time is short, and we are facing what I believe to be the most important election of our lives. If this gang gets another four years, they will dig this country into such a huge whole—financially, militarily, and diplomatically—that we will have to spend the next two to three generations digging ourselves out. We need to build an emergency "coalition of national unity," a big-tent movement that includes everyone from Green Party members and cranky leftists to mainstream Democrats and moderate Republicans.

You need to determine what part you can best play in this movement. Do you have money to spare to support a candidate for the presidency or Congress? Then do it.

Do you have personal and professional networks in "swing states" like Ohio, Michigan, Florida, Minnesota, New Jersey, West Virginia, Wisconsin, and New Mexico? Then use those networks. Send them letters, e-mails, call them on the phone; do whatever you need to do to make sure they're planning to vote, and that they understand that to a significant degree the future of our country is in their hands.

Are you active in your local church, synagogue, mosque, university, or community center? Consider sponsoring an educational event, or seeing if you can set up a candidate's forum where your local candidates for Senate or the House can be grilled on the issues. Are you a good writer? Then submit letters to your local paper early and often, expressing your views on the issues of the day, or critiquing their coverage of important matters of the day.

The most important thing in all of this is to find a way to *build activism into your everyday life*, at whatever level you are comfortable with. Some people may be so worked up that they take a leave from their jobs to campaign for the candidate of their choice. Others may take personal risks, like committing civil disobedience at the offices or factory of a local war profiteer. Still others may do the difficult but necessary work of trying to win over longtime friends, colleagues, or professional associates to the cause of taking back our democracy. The main thing to remember is that nothing is too little to matter. Democratic participation needs to become a habit, like getting exercise or good nutrition.

In my case, I'm a bit better at democratic participation than I am at *either* getting regular exercise *or* eating well, but hey, that's just me. I have the privilege of being able to work on foreign policy issues for a living, to be one of those "talking heads" you occasionally see drifting across the screen on *Fox News*, or CNN, or MSNBC. Whenever I do one of those shows, I think of my dad, Jack Hartung. My father was always yelling at the TV screen about the latest government outrage, or screaming about how the phone company was trying to screw us out of our hard-earned money, or otherwise giving a loud, running commentary on what was wrong with the world from his unique perspective.

My dad was by no means a progressive, but he had a healthy disrespect for governmental authority nonetheless. An accountant by profession, one thing my dad knew about was how to follow the money. His lifelong career as a conservative Republican—a guy who voted for Barry Goldwater, and who said that Nixon's biggest mistake was not destroying the White House tapes—came to a close in Ronald Reagan's first term, when he learned that Reagan was thinking of messing with the cost-of-living-adjustment (COLA) for Social Security. The dollars and cents finally prevailed over ideology, and at the next election, for the first time in my lifetime, my dad voted Democratic.

When I do my "talking head" bit on TV, I often think of my dad. Instead of being outside the TV shouting in, I have arranged a career in which I am occasionally the person inside the TV speaking out (or, if it's a Fox program, shouting out). There are lots of folks like my dad still out there in America—skeptical of government, reluctant to give it their money or their trust. We need to find the issues that will motivate some of these folks to join our emergency coalition of national unity and help send George W. Bush back to Crawford, Texas, where his tough guy act won't do quite so much damage.

What issue will move people into our camp? Maybe it's Bush's underfunding of his highly touted "No Child Left Behind Act," which is slated to get $10 billion less than promised this year alone. Maybe it is the Republican plans to partially privatize Medicare and Social Security, which are still firmly on the Bush agenda, even if he chooses not to stress it in the run-up to the election. Maybe it's the President's history of distorting the facts and diminishing the accountability that must be a central feature of a working democracy. Maybe it's Bush's opposition to a woman's right to choose, or his willingness to let the Justice Department snoop into our personal lives in the name of security. Maybe it's his hypocritical embrace of civil rights in theory, even as his administration's policies are undermining long-standing civil rights gains in practice. Or maybe it's the simple fact that if George W. Bush gets another four years in power, we may no longer have a democracy worthy of the name.

Because we live in America, we have a lot of advantages that people in other countries only dream of. We have more income, more spare time, greater access to independent news sources, and a system of free elections where, more often than not, the person who gets the most votes wins. These resources are not equally distributed, by any means, but most of us are far better off than our counterparts in other parts of the world. If we were trying to build democracy in Burma, or Saudi Arabia, or Uzbekistan, we'd be taking our lives into our hands. For most middle-class Americans, getting more active politically will at most cost us a little bit of aggravation or embarrassment, as our views clash with those of friends and acquaintances who are still buying the George W. Bush/Karl Rove mythology about the current occupant of the White House.

Whatever has kept us from raising our voices and mobilizing our friends and colleagues up to this point, we need to overcome it. From here forward, we need to try to live every day as if the future of our democracy depends on it—because it does. And, unlike picking up the garbage or fixing a leak in the kitchen sink, getting rid of the Bush regime is not something we can pay someone else to do for us. We need to roll up our sleeves and do it ourselves. *Then* we'll have a democracy worthy of the name, and we can put our heads together about how best to protect our nation, and the world. Our security is much too important an issue to be left to the likes self-serving ideologues like Richard Perle, Donald Rumsfeld, and Paul Wolfowitz.

Chapter 8 Notes

[1] For information on campaigns against war profiteering in Iraq, consult the web sites of the Institute for Southern Studies, at *www.southernstudies.org*; Global Exchange, at *www.globalexchange.org*; and the Nader group Citizen Works, at *www.citizenworks.org*. Taxpayers for Common Sense (*www.taxpayer.net*) has also done excellent work on the costs and consequences of privatizing the Iraqi occupation, as has Corpwatch (*www.corpwatch.org*). And, for fun, you should really check out *www.warprofiteers.com*, where veteran investigative journalist Pratap Chatterjee has put together an amusing and informative pack of war profiteer playing cards featuring everyone from Jay Garner and Dick Cheney on up to George W. Bush.

[2] Jonathan Weisman and Juliet Eilperin, "In GOP, Concern Over Iraq Price Tag–Some Doubt $20.3 Billion Needed for Rebuilding," *Washington Post*, September 26, 2003.

[3] On the Clear Channel/Bush connection, see Paul Krugman, "Channels of Influence," *New York Times*, March 25, 2003 (also available in Paul Krugman, *The Great Unraveling*, (New York: W.W. Norton, 2003), pp. 290–292).

[4] For more on contractors in Iraq, see Ceara Donelley and William D. Hartung, "New Numbers: The Price of Freedom in Iraq and Power in Washington," New York, World Policy Institute, August 2003.

[5] Chip Cummins and Neil King Jr. "New Office Created to Rebuild Iraq; Pentagon-Run Office to Award Contracts in Move to Prioritize Reconstruction," *Wall Street Journal*, October 14, 2003.

[6] Julian Borger, "Bush Cronies Advise On Buying Up Iraq," *The Guardian* (Manchester, UK), October 1, 2003.

[7] Edmund L. Andrews and Neela Bannerice, "Companies Get Few Days to Offer Bids on Iraq Work," *New York Times*, October 19, 2003.

—— ACKNOWLEDGMENTS ——

LET ME BEGIN by thanking my wife Audrey Waysse and my daughter, Emma Waysse Hartung, without whom none of this would have been possible. I am a better writer and a better person as a result of their love, support, and good humor.

Let me also thank my agent Anna Ghosh, of Scovil, Chichak, Galen, both for her help in promoting this book and for her patience in waiting for me to come up with a project worth promoting.

This book began with a conversation I had with Hamilton Fish at a reception in honor of the twenty-fifth anniversary of the John D. and Catherine T. MacArthur foundation, held at the Century Association in New York. As I frequently do at these sorts of events, I was working my way back toward the bar so I could be as far away from the speechmakers as possible, when who should I bump into but Ham. Ever the entrepreneur, he told me to think about whether I had a "Nation book" in me, pointing out that I could do well because I was probably among the top twenty-five writers that readers of *The Nation* magazine would recognize. I didn't exactly take this as high praise, given that on a good day I can't remember the names of twenty-five writers of any kind. But I took his invitation to heart, and filed away the idea that if I had a project in mind that would be "red meat" for progressives, I would run it by the folks at Nation Books.

Little did I know what a great opportunity Ham had offered me. Working with Carl Bromley and Ruth Baldwin, my editors at Nation Books, has been a pleasure from start to finish. They helped me hone down an interesting but long-winded manuscript into the lean, mean book you are holding in your hands. And they saved you a few hours of precious time, not to mention untold numbers of trees, in the process.

I have been a student of the military-industrial lobby for most of my adult life, so I am indebted to many people for the insights that appear here. First and foremost, I am forever grateful to Ceara Donnelley and Amy Frumin for devoting a good portion of the summer of 2003 to helping me track down news clips, reports, financial disclosure data, and other raw materials that went into the production of this book. My colleagues at the World Policy Institute's Arms Trade Resource Center, Frida Berrigan and Michelle Ciarrocca, were also extremely helpful at every step of the way, offering research assistance and encouragement as needed. I also benefited from the research of our former colleague Dena Montague, who has since left our little project to pursue a Ph.D at UCLA. My work on Lockheed Martin's Texas connections draws upon the intrepid research of my former colleague Jennifer Washburn. In addition, I would like to thank our director, Stephen Schlesinger, the editors of our journal,

Acknowledgments

Karl Meyer and Linda Wrigley, and my fellow Institute senior fellows Belinda Cooper, Michelle Wucker, Mustapha Tlili, Silvana Paternostro, and Sherle Schwenninger for their kind words and camaraderie along the way.

I am also thankful to the editors I have worked with most closely over the past few years as I have been writing on these issues, including Katrina vanden Heuvel and Karen Rothmyer at *The Nation*, Linda Rothstein at the *Bulletin of the Atomic Scientists*, Charlie Cray and Robert Weissman at the *Multinational Monitor*, Matt Rothschild, Sanhita SinhaRoy and Amitabh Pal at *The Progressive*, John Moyers and his talented group of editors at *TomPaine.com*, Jim Cason and David Brooks at *La Jornada*, Don Hazen, Lakshmi Chaudhry and Omar J. Pahati at AlterNet, and Noel Rubinton at *Newsday*. I have also been informed and inspired by the work of Jonathan Schell, in book and essay form, as well as in our occasional discussions of these matters.

My thinking has also been shaped by my interactions with my colleagues in the field, including Martha Honey, Tom Barry, John Gershman, Miriam Pemberton, Erik Leaver, and Emira Woods at Foreign Policy in Focus (*www.fpif.org*); David Gold, Kate Cell, Lucy Webster, Cindy Williams, Steve Kosiak, Carl Conetta, Charles Knight, Anita Dancs, Greg Speeter, Rob Manoff, John Schultz and Winslow Wheeler of the Security Policy Working Group (*www.cdi.org/spwg*); Gordon Clark, Kevin Martin, Tracy Moavero, Peter Fehrenbach, Ken Estey, and all of my friends and colleagues who are now, or once were, staffers for national or state affiliates of Peace Action; and Lora

Acknowledgments

Lumpe, Rachel Stohl, Natalie Goldring, Tamar Gabelnick, Matt Schroeder, Joe Volk, Bridget Moix, John Isaacs, Tom Cardamone, and all the other good folks who work or have worked with the Monday Lobby Group and the Arms Transfer Working Group in Washington, D.C. I also owe Ann Markusen many thanks for including me in the series of study groups she ran on military and economic issues at the Council on Foreign Relations from the mid-1990s onward, as well as for her seminal work in this field. I have benefited from the good work of my colleagues who have been keeping tabs on the Bush administration and its cronies, including Chuck Lewis and Bill Allison at the Center for Public Integrity; Medea Benjamin, Andrea Buffa, and all of their colleagues at Global Exchange; Keith Ashdown of Taxpayers for Common Sense; Rania Masri at the Institute for Southern Studies; Pratap Chatterjee, whose path-breaking analyses of Halliburton and other Bush-connected companies have appeared on the Corpwatch web site and in his dispatches for the Inter Press Service news service; and Charlie Cray and his colleagues at Citizen Works. For figuring out the neo-cons, I owe a particular debt to the work of Jim Lobe, Jason Vest, and John Judis. For thinking about the big picture, I always benefit from reading the essays and books of Michael T. Klare, whose writings originally inspired me to get into this line of work. For helping me understand "the lobby" in Texas, I am indebted to Robert Bryce. And for sheer clarity of thought on these serious matters, I have learned a great deal from the books and essays of my friend and colleague Rahul Mahajan.

Acknowledgments

Contrary to the general notion among progressives that the mainstream press is asleep at the wheel on these issues, I have learned a great deal from working journalists like Katie Fairbank of the *Dallas Morning News*; Tim Weiner, Paul Krugman, Thom Shanker, and Eric Schmitt of the *New York Times*; the late Mark Fineman of the *Los Angeles Times*; Doug Waller and Mark Thompson at *Time* magazine; Jonathan Alter at *Newsweek*; Greg Schneider, Dana Priest, John Mintz, and Michael Dobbs at the *Washington Post*; Julian Borger at the British *Guardian*; and Seymour Hersh at *The New Yorker*; to name just a few. Most important of all is Leslie Wayne of the *New York Times*—if there was a Pulitzer for "following the money," she would deserve to get it virtually every year.

I did this book as a citizen of this democracy who is concerned about its future, not as a representative of the World Policy Institute, or our home base, New School University, or any other organization. That being said, my ability to grapple with these issues has been greatly enhanced by the fact that for the past ten years I have had the privilege of working on issues of arms, the economy, and national security as the director of the World Policy Institute's Arms Trade Resource Center. During that period, my project has been sustained by a diverse group of foundations and individual donors that includes the Ford Foundation, the John D. and Catherine T. MacArthur Foundation, the Carnegie Corporation of New York, the Ploughshares Fund, the Compton Foundation, the CarEth Foundation, the Town Creek Foundation, the HKH Foundation, the Samuel Rubin Foundation, Rockefeller

Acknowledgments

Family Associates, the Deer Creek Foundation, Peggy Spanel, Mary Van Evera, Alan Kligerman, and David Brown. I am thankful to them for giving me the privilege of being a sort of professional gadfly, casting an independent eye on trends in U.S. foreign and military policy.

This book is dedicated to my dad, Jack Hartung, who put in five tough years of combat in the Pacific during World War II, fighting the war against fascism. My father was a lifelong Republican who voted for Barry Goldwater and thought Richard Nixon's only mistake was not destroying the White House tapes. But he was also an accountant, and some time in the early 1980s, when Ronald Reagan was thinking of messing with the cost of living adjustment (COLA) for Social Security, he started voting Democratic. At that point, he also came to have a greater respect and understanding for what I do for a living, and he was quite supportive in the early stages of my first trade book, *And Weapons for All*, which came out several years after he died. Despite our political differences, I am in many ways still my father's son, with the same healthy distrust of government and the same knack for weeding through budget estimates to get at underlying trends. I can only imagine what he would have thought of the shenanigans now going on in Washington under the guise of fighting terrorism. In his memory and in his honor, this book gives you my best take on what is being done in our name, and what we as citizens of a republic should be doing about it.

NEW YORK, NY
SEPTEMBER, 2003

INDEX

ABB, 59–60
activist organizations, 163–65
Adelman, Kenneth, 87 88
Air Force: bias for, 13–14; funding for, 73
Alexander, Lamar, 122–23
American democracy: actions needed to save, 159–70; protecting our, 166–70; threats to, by Bush administration, 156–59
American Enterprise Institute (AEI), 93, 103–6
Anti-Ballistic Missile (ABM) Treaty, 12, 56, 96
Armitage, Richard, 8, 10
arms industry: campaign contributions of, 3, 16–17, 129–33, 137–40; contracts awarded to, 119–22; jobs, loss of to overseas, xxi–xxii; mergers, 122–25; mergers in, 122–25; Paris exhibition of, x–xxii; profits made by, due to war on terrorism, 119–43; right-wing think tanks and, 98–103; salaries of CEOs in, 23–25

Bailey, Kathleen C., 100
Baker, James, 64–66, 76
Balkans, 31–33
Barker, Robert, 100
Bechtel, 34, 52, 86, 98–99, 155
Beckner, Everet, 136–37
bin Laden, Osama, 66, 151–52
Blackwill, Robert, 8, 10
Boeing, xi, xviii–xix, 119–21, 125–32

Bolton, John, 94, 103, 106–8
Brown and Root, 28; see also Halliburton
Bush, George H. W., 11, 64, 66–69
Bush, George W.: aircraft carrier landing of, xiv; Carlyle Group and, 70; connection of Lockheed Martin to, 133–36; conservative views of, 93; discrepancy between candidacy and presidency of, 4–7; foreign policy of, 11–21, 91–115; gaffes made by, during presidential campaign, 1–3; handling of crisis by, 148–49; influence of right-wing think tanks on, 93–115, 149; nuclear policy of, 19–20, 91, 94–100; power consolidation by, 156–57; propaganda campaign by, 157–58; support for, by arms industry, 3, 16–17

campaign contributions: by Halliburton, 34–35; by weapons makers, 3, 129–33, 137–40
Carlucci, Frank, 64, 66, 70–71
Carlyle Group, 16–17, 63–76; government connections of, 63–66, 68–71, 74; profits from war on terrorism by, 69–75; Saudi Arabia and, 75–76; Saudi Binladin Group and, 66–69
Center for Security Policy (CSP), 53–54, 56–58, 80, 93, 100–3
Chalabi, Ahmed, 88, 104–5, 153
chemical weapons, used by Iraq, 50–52